We recently lost our beloved pet "Bear," who was not only
our best and dearest friend but also the "Vice President of
Sunshine" here at Atlantic Publishing. He did not receive
a salary but worked tirelessly 24 hours a day to please his
parents. Bear was a rescue dog that turned around and
showered myself, my wife Sherri, his grandparents Jean,
Bob, and Nancy and every person and animal he met
(maybe not rabbits) with friendship and love. He made a
lot of people smile every day.

We wanted you to know that a portion of the profits of this
book will be donated to The Humane Society of
the United States.

–Douglas & Sherri Brown

THE HUMANE SOCIETY
OF THE UNITED STATES ©

The human-animal bond is as old as human history. We cherish our animal companions for their unconditional affection and acceptance. We feel a thrill when we glimpse wild creatures in their natural habitat or in our own backyard.

Unfortunately, the human-animal bond has at times been weakened. Humans have exploited some animal species to the point of extinction.

The Humane Society of the United States makes a difference in the lives of animals here at home and worldwide. The HSUS is dedicated to creating a world where our relationship with animals is guided by compassion. We seek a truly humane society in which animals are respected for their intrinsic value, and where the human-animal bond is strong.

Want to help animals? We have plenty of suggestions. Adopt a pet from a local shelter, join The Humane Society and be a part of our work to help companion animals and wildlife. You will be funding our educational, legislative, investigative, and outreach projects in the U.S. and across the globe.

Or perhaps you'd like to make a memorial donation in honor of a pet, friend, or relative? You can through our Kindred Spirits program. And if you'd like to contribute in a more structured way, our Planned Giving Office has suggestions about estate planning, annuities, and even gifts of stock that avoid capital gains taxes.

Maybe you have land that you would like to preserve as a lasting habitat for wildlife. Our Wildlife Land Trust can help you. Perhaps the land you want to share is a backyard — that's enough. Our Urban Wildlife Sanctuary Program will show you how to create a habitat for your wild neighbors.

So you see, it's easy to help animals. And The HSUS is here to help.

The Humane Society of the United States
2100 L Street NW
Washington, DC 20037
202-452-1100
www.hsus.org

Table of Contents

Introduction

Getting and enjoying wealth can add to the quality of one's life. While money and assets are not everything, they can have a powerful effect on the way a life is lived.

If you are the one that has earned your wealth, then you know that wealth does not come easily. You also have learned that it can be lost much more quickly than it can be gained.

Your own life may have been greatly enriched by your wealth, and you are now looking for ways to safely pass as much of it as possible on to those who will be your heirs. The number of your heirs may be increasing, making it even more important that as much of your wealth be preserved as possible through your remaining years.

Many tools are available to ensure that it goes to the ones that you want to receive it. No time should be lost, however, in placing your assets into those safe harbors where the troubles of life cannot harm it. An estate plan should be made to cover your assets as completely as possible to prepare for that inevitable day when the taxman comes looking to see what portion can be removed from your estate.

Estate planning is all about using the right tools. The job here is to transfer as much of your estate as possible to the hands of your heirs. Good estate planning will enable you to do this and greatly reduce your taxes, too. It can also enable your estate to last through multiple generations, depending on how large the estate may be.

In this book, you will find the tools available to convey your assets to future generations. Even better, you will find advice on what values must be passed on with them in order for your wealth to find the lasting value that you want it to have.

Section I

The Need for Estate Planning: Getting a Vision

You worked hard for many years to accumulate the wealth you have. You know exactly what it took to earn it, so it has more value to you than it does to others. You may now consider it a priority to enable your descendants to enjoy it.

You may see them, in your mind, being able to enjoy a better lifestyle with your money and other assets. You probably want them to be able to get a quality education and be able to enter into better-paying careers because of that education.

However, it may not be a good idea to simply hand a portion of your estate to each of them. Since wealth is power, you may also be able to use it to motivate, mold, or change young lives — especially among those who are going to receive it.

The need to transfer your wealth to others will come one day, and with it will come the wealth-devouring problems of taxes. Uncle Sam has devised many uses for your hard-earned dollars and other property — unless you apply various strategies to circumvent them.

That is what estate planning is all about — passing your wealth on to those that you want to receive it, and to do it with as little loss as possible. So now your vision takes on a new aspect — letting your heirs receive as much of your wealth as possible without it being siphoned off unnecessarily, especially when it can be avoided through a good estate plan.

1
Problems Typically Affecting Transfers of Wealth

No matter how well intentioned your plans may be to pass your wealth on to your loved ones, there are many potential roadblocks. Many of these roadblocks will go into effect if you do nothing to prepare your estate in the proper manner. Here are a few of the roadblocks that your estate planning needs to be prepared to handle.

A Lack of Proper Planning

The roadblocks present in one year may not be the same as the ones you may face in the following year. The applicable laws are constantly changing so that the average person cannot be expected to know all the details when preparations are made. This will require that you get assistance and guidance from a knowledgeable and experienced estate planner — one who knows the new laws and the ways to avoid possible problems.

Most people probably do estate planning with a will. While this is much better than not having a will at all, it often proves to be insufficient and may be easily contested, especially when a considerable amount of wealth is involved.

The problem here is not that a will is bad, but that it is of limited value when it is the only means of wealth transfer. No matter what other instruments you use, a will may still be needed to catch everything else, but it does not eliminate the dreaded estate taxes that other estate planning means could avoid.

Estate taxes can easily take away up to half of the wealth in an estate, and this is what will happen if you do not have some estate planning instruments in place to protect it. Taxes can usually be sidestepped through estate planning, which means that you get to pass that wealth on to others, and they can enjoy a much larger portion of it.

For the year 2007, the IRS allowed a single person to claim up to $2 million free from estate taxes. It is twice that number if you are married. If, in the event of your death, you want to transfer more than that amount to your loved ones, then you should plan on placing any amount above that into some form of estate planning. Greater amounts will be taxed at about 55 percent or more.

Another problem can occur if you leave all your possessions to your spouse. The good news is that you can still accomplish this without any estate taxes having to be taken out of the estate. If your vision ends with placing your estate into the hands of your spouse — with no taxes deducted — then you will have succeeded. The bad news, however, is that when the estate is passed from the spouse's hands into the hands of the children, there will be estate taxes collected. The heavy estate taxes have simply been delayed, not avoided.

Other problems can easily creep into simple planning of wealth transfer and upset those plans and intentions. While you make plans to give it to a daughter, it is quite possible that a no-good son-in-law could end up with all of it. A previous spouse could get your wealth, or a new spouse could give your hard-earned wealth to children from their previous marriage and leave your children without an inheritance. It can be hard to tell what might happen when it comes to money. Proper estate planning tools can lay a solid foundation and put your money where you want it to go — and could even keep it out of the hands of creditors.

There are estate planning instruments available that can help your estate avoid nearly all the taxes that consume so many other estates. It will take some planning and effort on your part to set them in proper order, but it will be worth it in the long run.

A Lack of Practice

Other problems can occur when you have agencies like the IRS carefully scrutinizing the organizational paperwork and practices of some of these estate planning structures. For instance, if a Family Limited Partnership (FLP) is not actually operating under the purposes for which it was designed, your FLP will automatically be declared null and void, and you will need to pay taxes on all the wealth placed under it.

In recent years, the IRS has put these organizations under a magnifying glass and is looking for faults. A number of people have found that they suddenly owed a large volume of taxes on their estate, simply because they did not fully understand how an FLP should operate and what limitations there are on the use of the assets placed in it.

In a number of these cases, though, it was the fault of the general partners (the original owners of the assets). Even though all the paperwork may have been correct, it was the daily operation that was at fault — even nonexistent — at least when it came to operating according to the plans. The IRS declares that, when these plans are not carried out, it is not a legitimate business and was obviously created merely for the purpose of tax evasion.

Other cases, however, showed that the estate planners themselves had failed to craft the organization with the care that should have been given to it. Loopholes and misunderstandings were the result, and this caused the problems in the long run, which resulted in a large portion of the estate being taken away in taxes prematurely.

A Lack of Understanding

Even if all the paperwork and organizations are in place and the proper format is followed perfectly, there is another major problem that still might exist. This problem, although not unforeseen, often remains untouched, and it quickly diminishes part of the estate and prevents that portion from being passed on to any succeeding generations. This problem concerns the attitudes and financial education of those receiving the inheritance.

If the recipients of the inheritance do not understand the value of the money and the property being given to them, then it surely will not last long enough to be given to their children. This seems to be the reason that some say wealth will not last more than three generations.

Good estate planning must first envision that the estate can be safely passed on to the descendants with a minimum loss to taxes and other problems. Second, proper care needs to be taken to ensure that, once estate planning has taken place, the practices needed to keep those instruments valid are fully performed. Third, care must be taken to ensure that the recipients are fully prepared to wisely use that inheritance so that their children and others can enjoy it too.

2
Preparations Needed to Meet Those Common Problems

Most of the situations mentioned previously can be avoided with good estate planning techniques. It will, however, take a well-thought-out plan that can be developed between you and the experienced estate planner.

As you take the time to consider the potential problems and where they might come from, they can be reduced or even eliminated altogether. Of course, there could be problems in the future that no one could possibly have foreseen, but good planning can reduce the threat in most cases.

Estate Planning Means Preservation

If you have nothing but a will to transfer your estate to your heirs, then most of your estate will go to Uncle Sam in taxes. In fact, everything in your estate above the $2 million exemption will be subject to at least a 45 percent estate tax (55 percent is possible). Unless you want all your hard-earned money to be given to the government, you must take your assets out of the reach of the taxman.

Even if you do not have more than $2 million in your estate, it can still be eaten up or taken away in part by unscrupulous means. That relative you wanted to leave out of your will might sue, or a family caregiver that was helping you could try to take most or all of it as recompense.

This is where effective estate planning becomes very useful to you. Proper estate planning methods literally take your assets and put them out of your estate — no longer touchable by estate taxes. Proper estate planning also puts your assets into an instrument that will make them more likely to be placed into the hands of those whom you want to receive them.

Furthermore, you have the opportunity to train and educate your family members and heirs in a way that will ensure that the inheritance lasts. Through a carefully devised program of education and checks, you may be able to ensure that the inheritance is enjoyed by more than three generations.

Qualified estate planners can look at your goals for estate planning and provide you with a solid approach for reaching your goals. They can help you see potentially weak areas and things that simply will not work for one reason or another.

Estate Planning Demands Careful Planning

Once you understand some of the things that may be done with your wealth, it will provide grounds for creating a vision. Your vision for the potential use of your estate becomes a basis for the way in which you will set up your estate planning. This is why you need to have the vision first, and then arrange estate planning to accomplish those goals.

In order to get started, you want to create and set down your vision for your estate and assets in writing. Remember that money and wealth are power and that estate planning puts you in a unique position to be able to make positive changes and influence the lives of your future heirs.

This influence could be both good and bad, depending on what the plans entail. Ask yourself questions like:

- What are your goals?

- How long would you like your estate to last?

- What are some definite objectives for the use of your estate once it is transferred?

- What preparations for the heirs should be made to help them be ready to receive and wisely use this wealth?

- What precautions need to be taken, and against what or whom?

- Are there heirs that may need guidance throughout their lives?

- What preparations do you need for yourself in your last days?

While these questions will give you a very broad overview as to the type of things you need to ask in order to develop your vision, they will get you started. The next chapters in this book will help you develop that vision further by showing you how you can use your estate to make a lasting impact on your heirs so that the wealth and its influence continue for as long as possible.

Estate Planning Means Problem Solving

Estate planning means that you foresee most of the possible problems and take them into account as you plan so that when problems arise, you can take them into consideration and make the necessary adjustments.

Preparing for problems, however, means that you will need to give considerable thought to the things that could happen — especially within your family. Every family is different, with different personalities and different goals. You will need to try to anticipate possible problems and prepare the plans and documents that will best allow you to accommodate those problems — or avoid them altogether.

In addition to the thought you need to give to this process is the advice and guidance you need from the experienced estate planner who knows what people are sometimes capable of and what the law may permit if there is a legal contest.

Attempts by outsiders, such as those who are guardians, husbands, or wives of those who are to receive the inheritance, or simply the irresponsible, should also be taken into account. This will require that you spend time with your estate planner in not only learning what might happen, but also in discovering ways to prevent things from happening that you never thought possible.

It is sad, but often true, that you never really know what a person is like until they are faced with the possibility of getting an inheritance. This motivates some to become very inconsiderate of other members of their family— even their own siblings or children.

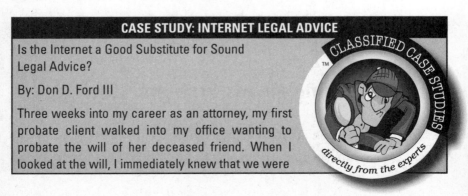

CASE STUDY: INTERNET LEGAL ADVICE

Is the Internet a Good Substitute for Sound Legal Advice?

By: Don D. Ford III

Three weeks into my career as an attorney, my first probate client walked into my office wanting to probate the will of her deceased friend. When I looked at the will, I immediately knew that we were

CASE STUDY: INTERNET LEGAL ADVICE

going to have problems. In fact, the probate of that estate was the longest-lasting probate case of my career.

The will was not a well-drafted one prepared by an attorney. Rather, it was a "do-it-yourself" downloaded will-maker package that the decedent had prepared for himself. In the 10 years since that first client came in, I have been reminded over and over again of the myriad of problems that arise when someone goes to the Internet for legal advice rather than consulting an attorney.

In my experience, most people look to the Internet and to will-maker kits because they think that it will be less expensive and easier than going to an attorney. Unfortunately, because of the problems that generally arise with these wills, what was intended to be a cost-saving measure generally results in increased hassle and expense to the client.

Will kits that are found either on the Internet or in office supply stores are generally not "state-specific." In other words, they are drafted so that they will try to comply with the laws of the majority of the states in the U.S. However, each state has its own specific requirements for what makes a will valid. In Texas, for instance, specific language must be included in the will to allow the court to appoint an executor as the "independent" executor. This important language makes the probate process in Texas much easier and less costly. Without the correct language, the family is going to end up expending considerable unnecessary time and expense in seeing the will through probate.

The other big problem that we have seen with these do-it-yourself wills is the fact that the person creating the will most likely does not completely understand all of the decisions that they are making in the will. As a result, we have seen several cases where the decedent said one thing in the will, but the entire family agrees that the decedent actually intended something other than what was said. These confusions occur because the decedent did not understand how to accurately express his wishes in the will, and in many cases, these confusions either create hard feelings among the family or end up producing litigation because the family is not satisfied with the likely unintended expressions of the will.

In another case, the decedent purportedly downloaded a will form from the Internet, and his wife believed that he had signed the form. However, she could only find the blank, unsigned copy after his death. When she came to my office, she could see no reason why she could not probate the unsigned copy of the will since it was the copy that her husband had downloaded from the Internet. Had she and her husband sought competent legal advice prior to her husband's death, they would have found out that the copy of the will was going to be invalid for disposing of the estate. In the end, she ended up having to expend much

CASE STUDY: INTERNET LEGAL ADVICE

more time and incurred significant expense in the probate of the estate, when it would have cost much less had they sought legal advice in advance.

In the year 1712, English poet Joseph Addison coined the phrase "a penny wise and a pound foolish" to describe someone who refuses to make a small investment on important items, instead choosing to unwisely spend large sums on unimportant things. Like the objects of Addison's description, choosing to consult the Internet for legal advice rather than employing a competent attorney generally marks unwise short-term savings that will likely produce long-term hassles and extra expenses.

Don D. Ford III is the Managing Partner of Ford & Mathiason LLP, a boutique estate planning, probate, and guardianship law firm serving Texas from offices in Houston and Dallas. Online at **www.ford-math.com**. 5151 San Felipe, Suite 1950, Houston, TX 77056.

3
Purposely Allowing for
Modifications in Your Plans

When you outline your vision in a plan that will meet the needs of the future, it is necessary to update it from time to time. This is especially true in our modern society.

Today, there are often many relational problems — people getting married, divorced, and remarried. To say the least, this means that an adequate estate planning tool may need revisions on a semiregular basis. This is even truer today if you have a large number of children and grandchildren included in your estate planning.

Often, young people may do their own estate planning by preparing a will. This is certainly one way to be prepared, but suppose that the original beneficiary was a previous spouse. A new spouse has come along, you have had three children together, and there are medical bills. What if all your possessions were left to the first spouse and nothing was left to your present family? Even though there was a will, it was never updated to name the new spouse and new children as the beneficiaries. In this case, the only way the second spouse might get anything would be to contest the will, and that could be costly in legal fees.

What would happen in the case of death is that the first spouse would get everything, possibly even the house the second family now lives in.

This could end up being a great tragedy and probably not at all what was intended. This shows why the documents that declare your intentions need to be kept up to date and why new family members need to be named as they come along.

Additional problems can be created, however, in the case of irrevocable trusts. While these are excellent tools to take your assets out of the tax man's reach, it is possible to end up with an undesirable situation that cannot be changed.

Assets can be left sometimes in the hands of one descendant. What happens if that descendant should pass away before the trustor? Or what if conditions are set forth in the documents and then never met?

Planning for your estate needs to involve a degree of flexibility, simply because you cannot foresee everything. Estate planners can help you see many things you might never have thought of otherwise, but even they do not know all things. It is essential that you work with your estate planner in the preparation of your documents so that you can cover those things you can predict. He or she may also be able to show you how to leave a little window so that you or the appointed trustee can make necessary changes in the future.

Being able to make some changes in the future, however small, could be enough to allow your estate planning to be successful for many generations. This is especially true in dynasty trusts — which can now go on indefinitely in some states. Who knows, in that case, what the needs of society or education or anything else will be 300 years from now? This degree of unpredictability demands that changes will be allowed to be made as they are needed by those who are faced with those problems.

This can probably be better understood if the situation is looked at in the reverse. Look back in history 300 years and imagine what it would be like if your inheritance were conditioned by one of your relatives who lived at the very end of the 17th century. Our world has become very different in that time.

Once your vision is set concerning what you can do with your inheritance, you simply want to leave some degree of flexibility in it. You should leave room for change, too, but not enough change that someone else can come along and alter your intentions.

Section II

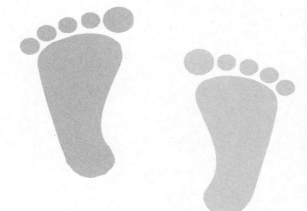

The Vision That Could Be Behind Your Inheritance

Taking your vision to the next level — beyond that of a basic goal — is the theme of this section. While some things were only hinted at in the first chapters to give you an overall idea, now it is time to go a little deeper. Here, you will be presented with some ideas that will help you determine what it may be possible for your heirs to do with your estate.

4
Setting Goals for Your Estate: What Are the Possibilities?

As you take a serious look at the wealth you have accumulated over the years, you (if you are first generation) can see some things that others cannot. No one else can understand the values you had that enabled you to get that wealth in the first place. Nor can others fully know what attitudes you now take toward those assets. It is these values and lessons that must be passed on to your future generations and that will enable the family riches to continue.

Interestingly enough, it is quite possible that those you intend to leave your wealth to may never have known what it means to be without it. Your children may have grown up enjoying the fruits of your hard labor and have possibly come to take it for granted. They may now mistakenly believe that it will always be there.

It is because of these attitudes in the successive generations that the lasting value of transferring wealth has problems. There is an old saying often referred to in estate planning books that says, "From shirtsleeves to shirtsleeves in three generations." Its meaning is still true today: those who have not learned either the value of hard work or how to appreciate those things that have not cost them anything are prone to spend and lose that wealth.

Unfortunately, in these cases, it may also be apparent that the successive generations may not have been taught how to continue to generate wealth or how to manage it successfully. Without this instruction, those who seek to transfer their wealth to the generation following may be doing so without hope of it ever reaching further generations. They may quickly find that it has been thrown to someone who is unappreciative of the work that went into getting it and who lacks the wisdom to know how to best use it or keep it.

If this pattern is ever to change, deliberate steps need to be taken to curb this waste. This change is what your vision needs to be about. It must include a way for your wealth to last more than the expected three-generation limit. Through the proper preparation and training of your children, the wealth can last much longer. But it will still only take one unprepared generation to spend the wealth — and then it is gone forever.

Several elements will be needed to prepare your children for the transfer of wealth to them. These elements should be looked at as goals to prepare your heirs mentally and intellectually to receive and properly use the wealth that they will be handed. Then their children will need to be trained so that these principles and values can be passed on to the next generation, which will then continue to spread them on to successive generations. Each of these target goals is listed here.

Family Closeness Is Needed

When family members get close to each other, there are several benefits. An appreciation for each other is one of the first. This appreciation is then transferred to the possessions that each one has. Once a family respects those that have created its wealth, they will treat their received wealth with a greater respect and want to honor the original owner. This is especially true if the descendants have fond memories of him or her.

Values Are Passed On

Family closeness should include not only time and activities together, but making decisions together as well. From this will come the passing of your values, and each family member will come to understand the processes that were involved in accumulating the wealth.

What may even be more important is passing on the worthwhile value of getting and having wealth. All too often, people with wealth perpetuate incorrect attitudes by simply handing money to their children without any instruction. Providing it on a mere whim encourages the belief that wealth is for their pleasure and spending, and there is no accountability learned.

Other means can prove far more valuable for ensuring that the family riches remain the riches of the family for many generations. You can start the process by educating the children. This means teaching them to handle money wisely, how to work for it, to appreciate it, to know how to invest and where, and even how to give it to worthwhile causes. Then you can make sure that the family riches are safe.

Decisions and Their Reasons Are Learned

When one individual makes the decisions, the thought process behind those decisions may not be transferred to those who are affected by those decisions.

The reasoning behind those important decisions can take place when there is some room for discussion. You can present financial problems or needs and then discuss them. Faulty thinking can be evaluated in front of other family members and then gently guided into a more correct position. In this way several things can be learned and accomplished:

- There is greater wisdom in a group than in one person

- Other people can have valuable insights that others may not have seen at all

- Each person can have a part in the decision-making process of maintaining family funds and the use of them

- Those who have excellent financial wisdom will be exposed and can be sought out when family members need counsel about their family financial decisions

Group Thinking Is Encouraged

When one person is making the decisions, the tendency may be for that one to think for selfish causes. When other family members are brought into the decision-making process, it becomes necessary for that person to take on a broader view. The presence of others will bring about decisions that are made for the good of the group as a whole. Thoughts that are narrow in scope will be exposed more quickly when the group is allowed to give input into the decision-making process.

Lessons and Stories Are Learned

As the family members are around each other, they will also learn the stories of the life of the originator of the family wealth. They will come to understand that:

- The wealth was not always there

- The wealth was gained by hard work

- There were some wrong decisions made

- Wrong moves can be overcome or corrected with better decisions

- Continued determination was behind the decisions to gain wealth

- Wealth had to be maintained with work — or lost

Future Goals Are Shared as Well

Among the many things that can be passed on by developing family closeness is the lesson that it will take deliberate and constant effort to pass family wealth on to children. Otherwise, it will simply not be there. Your heirs will need to know that they need to become as educated as possible, especially in areas of wealth building, as well as becoming committed to passing it on to the future generations.

A commitment will need to be deliberately made to pass those same values on to their children, who will pass it on. If one generation or family member fails in this aspect, then their portion of the estate will pass away with them.

5
Making Your Vision Last Longer Than One Generation: Why Stop With Your Children?

Communicating the need to be wise about spending is not enough. Rather, what is needed is an attitude that the wealth someone receives is not only his or her own, but that it also belongs to future generations. They are merely the channels through which that wealth must pass in order to get to their descendants.

This attitude of being a steward of something that is more than just money must be carefully passed down, along with all the tools and education needed to do the task. The family wealth needs to be approached as a business in which each family member not only has a part, but also a responsibility to do his or her part for the good of the whole.

The main reason it needs to be looked at as a business is because of where the family wealth is headed. While it took one or two to create the wealth in the first place, the first generation now knows that it must be divided between larger numbers as the children and their families increase. If there are three children in the first family, then each of them marries and could have two children. There are now nine ways to divide that same inheritance. Suppose that the following generation produces seven great-grandchildren (the fourth generation); the mere number of divisions necessary will destroy the riches quickly, and one or two family members cannot be expected to maintain it at the same proportion per family member. Thus, either everyone becomes involved or the wealth becomes destroyed because of the sheer number of people claiming a portion of it.

Creating a business attitude helps people stop looking at it as their own wealth. Most people understand that working for a business means that you must consider the benefit of the company above your own needs. That is the rule of the employee and all business partners.

The tendency of riches to become quickly dissipated is the result of several things:

- Each member looking out for himself or herself

- Limited vision of not seeing the impact that their selfish lives have on the next generations

- Failure to make corrections to maintain the often-dwindling resources

- Inability or unwillingness to prepare successive generations to build for the next one

- Failure to understand that maintaining existing wealth may take as much work as it did to create it

When those who first receive their inheritance can understand this, it is placed on their shoulders at that time to make corrections in the thinking of the family, if possible. Largely, this will be determined by the ages of the family members. Naturally, the younger they are, the more easily they can be taught.

Two steps are needed here: A plan must be developed and a commitment to that plan needs to be made by each family member. One or two of the senior family members need to carefully devise and present a means as to how the family can best continue the family wealth. Two things are necessary here. There needs to be some groundwork as to what constitutes a right and worthwhile use of the wealth, as well as clear means with goals as to how to maintain the wealth.

The plan then must also determine a way to inform, instruct, and involve the other family members as to the nature of the plan. This includes the fact that the family wealth is not theirs alone but belongs to the whole family and their descendants.

In the course of using this kind of method of preserving the family wealth, it is best if the family members come together to hear the presentation of the plan, as well as take part in the full development of it. The groundwork for the plan must start with a common set of values that the family holds to and is committed to clinging to through future generations. It is these values that will enable the family to work together and commit to each other. Then, the values will bring about the right perspective of the wealth.

After the values are set down, then a common meeting with the other family members needs to take place. The originators of the wealth should then present some of the following:

- The family history that brought those values to them

- Their own commitment to those values

- How those values enabled them to get and keep their wealth

- Their vision for the future and the continuation of those values with their attained wealth

Whomever the trend-setting family leaders are going to be in this endeavor, if not the wealth creators, they will need to have some good ideas as to how to go about the task. It will not be enough merely to tell others to increase the wealth of your family, but quality ideas will need to be presented, since some family members may not have a clue. Others may have already proven that they are not good candidates when it comes to handling finances. Nor will there be much time to waste developing a learning curve by experience alone. Excellent leadership, provided quickly, will help retain more family wealth than any other means.

By now, it should be obvious that making a plan to continue the wealth to more than one generation will not be easy. It is much easier to leave the wealth to your children and let them do with it whatever they want. However, it will not last this way past the third generation.

6
Deciding on the Heirs and Their Benefits: Why Waste Your Wealth?

How your wealth is divided up among your family members is entirely up to you. In light of what has been just presented, however, you may want to choose an alternate plan that will allow your wealth to go as far into the future as possible and to as many heirs as possible.

This means that you will need to become well informed as to what your options are and consider whether or not you want your heirs to have control of your assets or to simply have use of them after you are gone — as in a trust. Having the use of them will enable you to have a much larger degree of control over the assets, and it will also help them endure much longer.

You should also be aware that if you should die without a will, or having other plans in place, the state you live in has a plan of its own. Regardless of how you feel or of what you promised to whom, that plan will be carried out if there is no written plan in place.

This makes it mandatory that your plan be well thought out and just as carefully detailed on paper before you die. Hearsay is not going to count, and a document is always desired when something needs to be clarified.

When you choose the heirs to be included in your estate, you will need to give it much thought. Much of the thinking involves not so much who is to receive it, but in what form it should be given. For instance, if one of your children is a carefree spender and does not seem to understand the value of savings, then you may not simply want to give him or her cash. Your options could include a trust fund with a trustee overseeing the account.

Another child could possibly be somewhat mentally challenged and may not be able to make wise financial decisions. This will clearly require that someone guide the financial affairs of this individual.

A third situation that requires careful planning may involve your child who has married a financially irresponsible spouse who is also a spendthrift. You are concerned that he or she may try to get your child's portion of the wealth and waste it on frivolous things.

Another concern is that one of your grandchildren is addicted to drugs and uses all their money to support that habit. You are concerned that your hard-earned wealth may be used to further support the pusher rather than being put to good use.

Yet another concern could be that your second spouse would give your estate to his or her own children from a previous marriage and leave your earlier children without any inheritance at all. You, on the other hand, have different intentions.

Each of these potential problems requires a careful and thought-out solution that will allow you to place your assets into the hands of those you designate. Further problems may occur if you intend to leave someone close to you out of the estate plans altogether.

In each of these situations, you will need to decide whether to include the family member in question in your plans at all or to include them and provide some way around the obvious potential problems that each situation entails.

Besides these problems, you will also need to work to prepare the family for your decisions and attempt to predict where other possible problems could arise. For example, will so-and-so feel left out and attempt to grab their perceived portion of the estate?

Before you exclude someone from the estate, however, it may be a good idea to learn what kinds of estate planning tools are available. It may be possible to let that person "use" the benefits of the estate without actually consuming it or spending it. This way, you reduce the possibility of that part of your estate being abused and lost due to a lack of proper diligence.

As you list each of the beneficiaries — all your children, stepchildren, grandchildren, nieces, nephews, and so on — you want to make sure you have them all. Do not forget to add your spouse in there, too. This way, you know whom you are dealing with and how many.

In most states, there are laws that work in favor of those who have been removed from a will or other estate planning device. This means that, if you do not intend to put someone into your will at all, you should first be aware of what the law in your state declares so that you can work around it. Otherwise, you are simply asking for trouble. For instance, if you leave your spouse out of the picture altogether, most states say that he or she has the right to a portion of it, thus guaranteeing them sustenance. By neglecting him or her, you may just have caused the whole will to be rewritten, and your plans may become null and void.

Next, you can start deciding which special assets you want your heirs to have. You can also jot down some quick notes as to what kind of special needs an heir may have in the way of finances. Does he or she need some specialized education to bring them up to par, such as becoming capable of wisely handling the inheritance? This is where you can sit down and begin to make your vision a tangible thing. Write down things like:

- What goals do you think would be good in the way of character development?

- What business-knowledge development does he or she need?

- What about the development of his or her ability to handle finances?

- What talents does he or she possess that could be further enhanced?

If he or she is too young, such as may be the case with grandchildren, then you would also need to make plans for a trust fund with possible guardians appointed to watch over the estate until no longer needed. You will also need to decide what would constitute the conditions under which a guardianship may no longer be needed.

If you believe that a particular heir would be inclined to spend his or her money recklessly, then you can place more stringent rules governing the use of the assets given. If you intend for a particular child to be in charge of much of the estate — say, as a trustee — then you may want to provide special financial training or experience for that one. More ideas will be presented in the following chapters.

Leaving a child or grandchild out of the will completely could be a problem if you do not take deliberate steps to prepare for it. Probably the worst thing you could do is not mention the child in your will at all. This would provide leverage for the angle that you intended to leave something to him or her but simply forgot when you wrote out the will. Instead, you want to mention him or her by name, more than once, and possibly why you decided not to leave a portion of the inheritance to him or her. This would prove that you did not accidentally forget.

This should give you some ideas as to what you can include when choosing your heirs. You should also include any instructions or descriptions as to how to use the inheritance wisely.

The vision is yours alone. With the right tools at your disposal, combined with the fact that heirs naturally want an inheritance, you are in the driver's seat — all you need to do is see the potential.

Section II

Taking Inventory of Your Vision's Assets

When you begin to think about passing your wealth on to your descendants, it becomes necessary for you to know exactly what wealth you have. You should put all your assets down on paper or in a spreadsheet so that everything can be included in your estate planning. It is important that you remember that whatever is not included will most likely be covered by your will, or not at all, and will need to go through probate, in which you may lose a large portion to probate costs and estate taxes.

Taking this step, you may find that you have more wealth than you realize or not as much. It is also possible that you cannot pass on some things you thought you could.

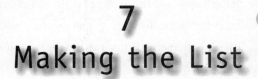

7
Making the List

Your assets will start out with those things that are in your name, meaning that you are the named owner.

Here are some things that come under the various types of property you own:

- Real estate — This includes land, homes (including your own), business property, and rental properties

- Cash — Actual cash, bank accounts, and savings

- Investments — Stocks, CDs, bonds, and mutual funds

- Retirement funds — 401(k)s, IRAs, annuities, and other special retirement funds

- Insurance — Life and other types

- Business ownership and investments — Partnerships, businesses owned, and joint ownerships

- Special collections — Art, coins, stamps, cars, and jewelry collections that are out of the ordinary and of special value

- Vehicles — Cars, sport vehicles (like ATVs and jet-skis), boats, aircraft, tractors, antique vehicles, and farming equipment

- Miscellaneous — This category includes most everything else that would be found in the house, such as furniture, computers, office equipment, libraries, appliances, clothing, guns, and tools

It is not necessary to list those things you use every day. Things like your clothes do not really need to be listed, except those that are of special value, such as leather coats or suits.

As you make out your list, it is a good idea to list everything that has special value. In many cases, you will want to make sure that a particular son or daughter gets specific items. You could make a checklist for yourself when you give these things away or include them in your will, saying which children or grandchildren are to get what items.

After you have created the list, you should determine as closely as possible what the actual value of each item is. For the more valuable items, you may need to get an appraiser — especially for any real estate, antiques, or pieces of art and jewelry.

You can determine the value of other items you own by looking on the Internet and seeing what they are selling for. One good place to do this is **www.ebay.com**, where you can get an average asking price for that particular item. Another good place to go is a store that sells used items and check on the price they are going for there.

It is an excellent idea to take pictures of each valuable item so that there is no question later about what it is you are actually giving to others. Another option is to film your possessions as you go from room to room and discuss the items of particular value. You may want to actually mention the value of the item, as well as a little history of it, in the video.

Once a thorough list has been created, you want to put it all in one place so things can easily be settled when needed. This means you need to list all bank accounts, savings accounts, stocks, bonds, CDs, life insurance policies, and the like so that they can easily be made a part of the estate or distributed as planned when the time comes. Your relatives should not have to use legal means to discover where your assets are. This could be very costly and time consuming.

You should also have money set aside and available for your funeral expenses when you pass away. Since all your other assets may not be immediately accessible to your family members, cash will be needed for these expenses, which could be as high as $10,000. These expenses, however, can often be prepaid with certain funeral homes in order to make those difficult times a little easier for your loved ones.

8
Adjusting the List

S ome things cannot be added to the list, even though you have an investment in them. Primarily, this includes those things on which you hold a joint interest. As long as someone else's name is on a deed, investment, or any other asset, then technically you are not the owner. This means that you cannot put it in your will or other estate planning instrument.

Although the money or property invested in a joint ownership is yours, you do not own the whole of it; therefore, you can only pass on the right to that portion. Joint ownership property could cause problems when it comes to transferring property, unless it is to your spouse or to whoever is the joint owner. For one thing, a joint ownership situation supersedes a will, meaning that even if the property is mentioned thoroughly in your will, any joint ownership agreement will stand in most places. This makes the will of no value when it comes to that particular asset.

Some will try to use a joint ownership as a means to bypass estate taxes. It will successfully accomplish that. However, that is about all that can be guaranteed. Since the partner legally becomes the owner, it only makes sense that he or she now has the right to do with it as desired. He or she is not legally under any further obligation to carry out anyone else's wishes or verbal agreements and could decide to pass it on to his or her own descendants.

This means that if you put your house into the joint ownership name of one of your children and entrust them with the responsibility of selling it later and dividing up the money with his or her other siblings, he or she does not have to do it. Anytime you have a joint ownership, the other named party actually becomes the full owner when the other named party dies. For this reason, it is probably a good idea to use another means to transfer large items without using joint ownership.

Care also needs to be taken if you have financially or materially blessed one of the heirs more than the others. This means that if you have paid for your son Johnny's education to become a lawyer but did not do so with his older brother and younger sister, there may be sufficient cause for legal action when the will is read.

Even though it may not have been thought of at the time, others may become acutely jealous of Johnny because they did not receive what they might consider an equal portion of your estate. So, while you are going to try to divide it up equally, the other siblings may assume that part of it has already been distributed and they were not in on it. Unless Johnny decided to pay it back, you may talk to the heirs to see how they feel about it before you finish your estate planning.

From your estate totals, you will need to subtract all existing debt. Whether it is mortgage payments, business debt, credit card debt, loans, or anything else, it must be subtracted from the overall value of the estate. In addition, any debt owed to the wealth creator will also need to be included.

After all your debt is subtracted, you will have an accurate value of your estate. From this figure, you can calculate what is needed for your future and what you hope to have to distribute once you are gone.

9
Tuning the List

After you have completed your list, it is time to decide how you will distribute your estate and to whom. There are several ways you can help to ensure that the best person will get what he or she deserves.

For your personal items, you may simply ask your loved ones whether there is something special they want or have an interest in. Ask them to put it in writing and then you can compare notes. It might actually surprise you what is of value and interest to some of them. Then you can decide whether there is a conflict and to whom you will give each item.

If you should wait until after you are gone to give away the items, then make a notarized list and give a copy to each heir. This makes the list legal, and since each heir will have the same list, there really can be no question about who is to get each item. If they change their minds later, they can swap gifts for something else they are more interested in — if someone else is willing to exchange.

For larger items, you can do the same thing, if you are not already aware of your heirs' interests. Of course, when you ask for their opinions and interests, you may be surprised by the answers.

10
Keeping the List Current

As you look over the various assets that you have, it is important to remember that the list will change. This means that it must be updated from time to time so that it reflects the actual assets you possess. When you add more possessions to your estate, they will need to be placed under some means of estate planning other than a will, so that they do not need to go through probate.

Changes in your life are another reason updates need to be made. All too often, documents are left unchanged. Later, when needed, the intended heirs find that all was left to a previous wife or some such thing.

Other problems could be caused in the case of heirs who are now deceased. An inheritance that was going to a daughter, now deceased, will become the property of her husband who may not know how to control money. In a case like this, if the money were placed in a trust, then at least the children could get to enjoy some of it.

Even potentially more hurtful would be a grandchild that is born later and is left nothing. While it may have simply been an oversight, after your death it obviously is too late to redistribute the wealth to include this child. Even if others do consider it a mere oversight, however, there still can be hurt feelings — and no wealth for him or her.

If you end up with a list that does not match the assets, an uneven distribution of your assets could easily occur. If some assets were sold prior to your death, or given away, then the distribution becomes uneven, providing ground for trouble between the intended heirs.

Consideration also needs to be taken for additional expenses, like the cost of:

- Maintaining the estate through the years

- Funeral expenses

- Living expenses for the remaining spouse

- Inheritance taxes

- Bills

- Last medical expenses

- Probate costs

All these will need to be paid for out of the estate before it can be closed and all transactions finalized.

11
Protecting Your List

O nce you have your list complete, then you know what you are really worth. In order to ensure that most of this wealth actually gets into the hands of your loved ones, you want to make sure it is properly insured.

This will require looking over your various insurance policies to make sure that they cover your current assets. Normally, as you get older, you accumulate more possessions or property, and you may have some that are not yet insured. You will need to talk to your insurance agent to make sure that everything is brought up to date, which will probably mean an increase in your insurance premiums.

Updating your insurance should be done on a yearly basis just to reflect the value that needs to be covered. Especially in times when the value of real estate is fluctuating often, you neither want to be paying too much in premiums (if housing values in your area are dropping), nor do you want to be underinsured if your properties are increasing in value. You also do not want to have less insurance than you need if you have gained more valuable assets not yet covered. Items that are of special value, such as paintings, antiques, and jewelry, need to be separately appraised and insured.

As you consider the future of your estate, it is a good idea to see what might take place. If you are planning on making any purchases, you need to remember that this will reduce your estate. This may mean that each of your heirs will now receive less money or assets, unless the income from the estate is larger than these expenses.

If you are expecting any other major changes in your estate, you need to recalculate and make the necessary adjustments so that the heirs still will get an approximately equal portion of your estate, if that is your intended plan.

Section III

Choosing the Right Tools to Carry Out Your Vision Successfully

After you have established your vision for your wealth and its ability to positively influence your children and other descendants for good, you will need to select the tools you need to get the job done. You will need to familiarize yourself with the various tools to determine which one will best accomplish your purposes, but doing so will be well worth it. Do not forget the value that an estate planner can provide in helping you to design the best program for your wealth transfer.

Although a number of reasons could be given as to why you should know these estate planning tools, the main reason is so that you can make wise choices. Beyond that, you will need to be able to tell your children and grandchildren that understanding how estate planning works is not so difficult.

It is better that you help make the choices for your estate plans along with the estate planner, rather than let the estate planner make all those decisions for you. You will come up with a better strategy and practical plan when you provide questions and input, and help in designing the right plan to fit your needs.

You will need to get some assistance from more than one expert in order to make the best decisions, but your knowledge about what is involved is necessary in order to detect when an estate planner is simply trying to use the easiest process for him or her. Developing a quality estate plan that will allow your heirs to preserve your estate for more than three generations will largely depend on what tools they are given. Poor planning on your part may only force your heirs to sue so that they can get control, and then they will have it their way.

This section will focus on the various tools at your disposal so that you can pass your wealth on successfully to several generations. The benefits of each are included, as well as some potential pitfalls for you to avoid.

12
The Will

The will is probably your most essential document in estate planning. Although it is your plan to place as much as you can outside your will, it will serve as a backup document for everything else. Since a will is quick to make and change, it is suggested that you have a will prepared immediately to cover your basic desires. This way, in case you should die before the estate is properly planned — which could take months — at least your desires are in print and can be carried out. This will not allow your estate to escape probate and estate taxes, however, but it will go where you want. This also means that it will stay away from those you do not want to have it.

You Need a Will First

Having a basic will until your estate gets placed in the position you want it only makes sense. Remember that if you die without a will, the state then proceeds to distribute everything according to its own plan.

Once the rest of your estate planning is set up, you can easily change your will. If you should set up the estate and then die before you have time to change the will, your estate planning will go into effect. The will becomes overturned concerning those portions of your estate covered by other estate planning means.

It should also be pointed out that, if you do not have a will, the state automatically becomes your heir. This is not a pretty picture for your valuable assets since now a much larger portion of your estate will probably be lost. It means that:

- There is no executor; the court will have to be appealed for one.

- There are no guardians for your children; one will be appointed for them.

- No money will be given to any charity or other organization of your choice.

- Your estate will be divided between your spouse and your children.

You can see that this is not a good way to go. It would be a waste of time and money not to get that will immediately, considering what is at stake.

Something that is just as important, however, is that you use a lawyer to help you with the will. While it is possible for you to write your own, it will be more likely to stand if you get legal help. Such a document needs to be prepared to withstand any onslaughts that might come against it. The larger your estate, the more likely it is that this could happen. Legal language that you, as a nonlawyer, might use could take on an entirely different meaning you did not intend, or it may accidentally leave more room for interpretation than what you want. Professional legal counsel can enable you to overcome this obstacle by using precise legal terms.

Conditions for a Legal Will

A will needs to have several conditions in place before it is deemed a valid document. If any one of these conditions can be disproved, then the will is not going to be recognized as a legal representation of your will. Instead, it will be thrown out and then your assets become subject to the will of the court. This makes it imperative that you meet the requirements exactly when completing your will.

In order for a will to be considered legal, there are three conditions:

- You must be of a sound mind; you understand your assets and plans for them.

- You must be at least 18 years old (may vary in some states).

- You must have two witnesses; they cannot be heirs and must both be present at the same time and sign the dated document. At least one state now requires three witnesses.

While those are the basic requirements, it is also essential that there be some property listed on it and an executor appointed. Besides that, a will has no purpose unless a beneficiary is also named.

CASE STUDY: LAW OFFICE OF ALAN H. SEGAL

175 Highland Ave.
Needham, MA 02494
Tel: 781-444-9676
Fax: 781-444-9974
Email: alan.segal@segallawoffice.com

Every adult who owns property or has minor children should have an estate plan or at the very least a will.

If you do not have a will, the state writes one for you.

CASE STUDY: LAW OFFICE OF ALAN H. SEGAL

The state controls who gets your assets, who runs your estate, and who cares for your minor children. Even for people who own assets in a living trust, a will is still crucial to catch any assets that may be outside the trust, or may be created at death, and pour them into the trust. More detailed estate plans are recommended depending upon the value and types of your assets. In addition, a healthcare power of attorney is used to express your medical wishes and state who you want to make healthcare decisions if you are unable to. This gives your agent very important authority and gives this important responsibility to the person of your choice rather than a person chosen by the healthcare provider or state law. As most states have their own standard forms, it is wise to have a valid power tailored to the state that you are currently living in and to update it when you move. Once the documents have been signed, it is important to have an accessible place for them to be found. A common problem we come across is persons who have lost or misplaced their original executed documents. This problem is especially crucial when it comes to your will. As a general rule, only the original executed will can be admitted to probate. This presumption may be overcome by strong evidence proving a contrary intent, but this can be a tricky proposition and not one you want your heirs to rely on. The best location for the original will is a safe deposit box. The next best option is a fireproof home safe.

In either case, it is important to let your family know where they can find the documents when they need to locate them. Powers of attorney should not be stored in a safe deposit box because they may be inaccessible when needed on a holiday or weekend. When we prepare and execute documents, we provide clients with specific instructions on how and where to store them.

My office is presently dealing with a client who is enduring the burden of improper and inadequate estate planning. The client is a 52-year-old disabled person. His mother owned the house that he lives in and died in 1989. The mother had a will that left the house in a trust with a trustee appointed to handle the costs and expenses dealing with the house and the power to mortgage or sell the house. As it turns out, my client and his sister did not get along and she moved from Massachusetts to Mississippi. There was no mortgage on the house, but since my client was on a low, fixed, Social Security disability income, he had a difficult time paying for the upkeep of the property and the real estate taxes. The town where the property was located sent many notices of delinquency regarding the real estate taxes and finally decided to foreclose on the tax lien. My client decided that the only way to keep the property was to get an equity loan from a bank to pay off the tax bill. Unfortunately, the loan could not go through because the sister who was a joint owner of the property refused to sign the loan papers and refuses to discuss anything about the house. Had the deceased mother expanded her estate plan to include putting the house in a trust, this problem could have been avoided. The appointed trustee would have had authority to mortgage the property and the house could be saved. Now, in order to rectify the situation, we are proceeding with a petition to the court to partition the property by having the court appoint an independent person to determine the value of the property and to sell the property in order to pay off the real estate taxes to the town and to give my client and his sister their rightful share of the equity. This will be expensive and time consuming and could have been avoided.

I have another client that did follow my advice with his estate plan and was able to save his estate a significant amount of money. Some states, including Massachusetts, have an estate tax on estates that are valued at more than a million dollars. That sum is fairly easy to get to when you add in the value of your home, stock investments, and life insurance.

Yes, life insurance proceeds are considered part of your estate for estate tax purposes. I helped save the estate money by transferring the house and all of his assets from his name into a family trust with his family members as beneficiaries. That technique avoided the probate process and saved the costs associated with attorney fees, court costs, and advertising costs (you know, the ones you see in the local newspapers). It also had the benefit of shielding the listing of his assets in court for any member of the public to view. After explaining all this to my late client's surviving heirs, it served as a lesson to them to do proper estate planning in order to spare their children the costs of probate and make sure that their assets pass to their children in the most financially favorable manner.

Types of Wills Available

To make it convenient for a will to be written, there are now a number of different types available. These include everything from the time-tested paper will to the holographic will. Some of them have specific purposes or situations in which they can be used; others simply allow you to choose. Before you have a will made, however, you should check to see which types are allowed in your state. It may even be possible that your state will not permit a handwritten will or other types. Under some conditions and in some states, you may use a holographic will, which is handwritten and requires no witnesses.

Overall, there are six primary types of wills. Following is a brief overview of each.

Simple Will

This will describes the basic things you want in a will. It names your property, your beneficiaries, and what you want them to have. It will also appoint an executor of the will and possibly a secondary. You can also name someone to be the caretaker of your children, a charity that you want money to go to, and any other special instructions you have. It is a will for only one person.

Holographic Will

This is a will that has been handwritten. Many states (about 30) no longer accept this kind because it can be forged. It is better if you go through legal channels and have it done right to avoid questions and risk having it declared a forgery.

Pourover Will

This type of will places some of your assets into a trust or similar structure when you die. The trust or other instrument will need to have been previously created.

Joint Will

This document is for husbands and wives to fill out together. Problems with this document can arise, however, because they are often declared unchangeable. This could be very harmful, especially if the surviving mate remarries and has children. The main problem is that all property passed to the surviving spouse becomes theirs, and then he or she is free to do with his or her property as desired. This means any stipulations about giving any possessions to anyone else may never happen. He or she does not have any obligation to fulfill it. It is better if there are separate wills for each.

Testamentary Trust Will

This will creates a trust for some of your assets after you die. It appoints a trustee and names beneficiaries. Terms for receiving benefits from the trust are given and often an income is appointed. More than one trust can be created in the same will. This type of will could be created to take care of a child that may never be able to be independent and self-supporting.

Oral Will

This one is also called a "nuncupative will." The oral will permits a person on his or her deathbed to make a last-minute will, when there is no time to do it any other way. Most states, however, do not allow it.

Other Wills

There are a few other types of wills that are sometimes permitted. Here are several more:

Ethical Wills — This will is a good choice if you want a chance to share with your remaining descendants a little history, some of your thoughts, or a piece of your mind. You can even tell them why they are not receiving anything in your will. It is usually accompanied by a traditional will. You could also provide conditions on an heir receiving an inheritance, such as graduating from college.

Mutual Wills — This type of will could be made between one or more partners working on a single project. A part of the partner's money could be willed to be donated to the project in the event death comes before its completion.

Electronic Wills — This is something that will probably be more prevalent soon, but right now only Nevada accepts an electronic will. Strict verification procedures have to be followed in order to certify that a particular person wrote it.

Living Wills — This is not actually a will, but is designed to let doctors and family members know what your intentions are concerning being maintained by life-support machines if you become terminally ill or comatose.

Video Wills — These are becoming more popular today, but you should not rely on one to effectively convey your assets to others. Generally, they should only be used to provide a backup to a written will and as a way to prove your intent as well as sanity at the time it was made.

It also needs to be pointed out that prewritten will forms and similar things are available in stores or online. The potential problem here is that they may not meet your state's requirements. They also may not be as flexible as you may need them to be to accomplish all your estate planning goals. This means that, by using these forms, you take the risk that your will may not be a legal document in your state, which essentially could leave you without a will.

Using the legal services of a lawyer for your estate planning will help you sleep at night, knowing that it has been completed according to local law. Your children and spouse will also sleep better. While it may cost a little more, it will cost you far less than the estate taxes imposed if your will is declared null and void.

Making Changes to Your Will

Once your will is written, it can easily be changed by either making a new one or by a codicil. A codicil is an amendment to an existing will, which makes alterations simpler than rewriting the whole will. Professionals should also word codicils to ensure that proper legal language will successfully accomplish your desires in court.

It is important that your new will make all other pre-existing wills void. This makes it clear that this is the only one that matters.

Things That You Cannot Put in Your Will

Part of estate planning involves taking most of your property out of your will, which means that it will not go through probate. You must put those assets somewhere, so you will create other instruments to place them into. Once an asset is put into another instrument, you cannot put it into your will as well. Here are some more specifics.

Joint Property

Anything that you possess in joint or partner with someone else cannot go into a will. The main reason is that you are not the sole owner, and therefore, have no right to give it away. These items can be mentioned in other instruments and dealt with properly there. Any reference to this type of item in a will is simply going to be overridden by what the other documents declare.

Items That List a Beneficiary

If you have preselected a beneficiary for some of your specific assets, then you do not need to put that into your will. Again, it will simply be ignored. This includes anything that names a beneficiary, such as life insurance policies, Individual Retirement Accounts (IRAs), 401(k)s, or anything else.

Payable on Death Accounts

For some things, like bank accounts, you may have been allowed to fill out a form identifying someone as the recipient in the event of your death — commonly called a payable on death account. This means the account is automatically placed into the possession of whoever is named, such as a beneficiary, when you die. Some stocks and bonds may also be in a similar situation, and these are usually called transfer on death accounts. The named recipients (beneficiaries) can easily be changed, if needed, by filling out a new form. It is important to check to see who is named every now and then, and then update it if needed.

Living Trusts

These instruments are also outside the jurisdiction of a will. Any property you have identified in a living trust does not need to be mentioned in your will.

Funeral Information

In most cases, your funeral will already have taken place before a will is ever read. In some cases, it will not even be found beforehand. The execution of a will can take many months and sometimes years before fully complete. Any funds to be used for funeral expenses and taxes on the estate should be kept separate for that purpose. It is recommended that you prepare a separate letter expressing your desires for burial.

Any other details concerning your funeral and related arrangements should all be included in this document. You can include any details you think your family would want to know. This can include whether your organs are to be donated, whether you want cremation, whether you want your ashes spread somewhere, who you want your pallbearers to be, the details of the funeral ceremony, and anything else you think is important. The choice is yours.

Placing Personal Items in Your Will

It is common to name items of value and designate the beneficiaries by name in your will. In fact, this is very important if there are children from more than one marriage. This is about the only way to make sure some of your heirlooms and other valuables can be left to each.

This does require, however, that you be as clear as possible when identifying both the beneficiary and the gift. Mentioning something by the term "diamond ring" could be of little value if there is more than one diamond ring. If you describe it unmistakably, then there is little room for dissension among the relatives. A video that actually shows the item could help identify the gifts in mind.

Naming Your Heirs

It goes without saying that your heirs need to be identified. However, many problems arise from the fact that the list of heirs can quickly change. New ones can come along and other ones can pass away. If you designate an heir and he or she passes away, do you intend for his or her children to receive the inheritance intended for the deceased? What if there are no children?

Once again, this requires further thinking and planning — and then putting it into your will. Each heir should have a replacement — and so should your gifts — in case something is lost or sold. This also applies if you wish to leave money to a charity or other organization. Since any organization could also become nonexistent over the years, you should either name a potential second organization, a type of organization that you leave to the discretion of the executor of the will, or what to do with the gift otherwise.

Naming a Guardian for Your Children

In the event of your death, and the death of your spouse, it is very important that you provide for the future arrangement of your children. This means that you need to appoint a guardian suitable for the task.

When making the selection for a suitable guardian, you want to find out:

- Whether they are willing

- Whether they can financially manage it

- Whether the new home is suitable for the children

You can avoid potential conflicts of interest if you do not choose the executor of your estate and the guardian of your children to be the same person. Otherwise, they may decide to use some of the estate in the name of the children to build their own estate in some way.

While it is a good idea to designate that a maintenance allowance be used if it is needed, this should be limited so that a larger portion remains when the money could be most needed and preserved. Be sure also to choose an alternate guardian in the event that your first choice change their minds or become divorced.

Giving Your Executor the Needed Powers

When the will is written, it is very important that certain powers be clearly laid out for the executor. These powers may be necessary in order for him or her to adequately handle the affairs of the estate while it is under his or her authority. This may include the power to sell some of the assets in order to pay bills or taxes, as well as the possible need to borrow against the estate, as opposed to necessarily having to sell it in order to get needed funds.

The alternative to this is that the executor may have to go to court first in order to get those same powers. Obviously, the cost to do this will come out of your estate anyway, and the time needed to accomplish this could stretch the settlement time needed considerably.

When to Change or Update Your Will

Since a will is the means to transfer your wealth to your heirs and fulfill your vision, it needs to be updated when major changes take place in your life or when heirs need to be added or subtracted. A will should be looked at as being flexible up until you pass away. As you accumulate more assets, this should be reflected in your will.

Another time to change your will is when you move from one state to another. Since the rules may now be different, your will needs to be adjusted to suit the new ones. In some states, the rules may be vastly different. If you move into a community property state (which includes the western states of Arizona, California, Idaho, Nevada, New Mexico, Washington, and the central states of Louisiana, Texas, and Wisconsin), half of what you earned during the marriage belongs to your mate. This means that he or she can choose to do with it as he or she sees fit. The only exception would be if a prior agreement had been made that would nullify this effect. Other states entitle a spouse to anywhere from one-fourth to one-third of the estate gained in the marriage. In order to get a larger portion, though, the will would need to be contested in court.

When you have marital changes, it is a very good time to review all the documents for your estate. You will want to be sure to change the beneficiaries on your life insurance, retirement funds, investments, bank accounts, and more. If you should still have an ex-spouse on your will when you pass away, in nearly all cases the courts will discount it. This is not true, however, in other documents in which the ex-spouse may be named as the beneficiary, such as with a life insurance policy.

As an added precaution, though, there is another, surer way to make sure that your ex does not get anything. Simply rewrite your will and make sure it states that all previous wills are null and void.

As you update your will from time to time, you will want to check with your selected candidates for guardians for your young children to see if they are still interested. Attitudes can change with time, or their own situation may change.

You will also want to make sure that you have a separate will for any property held outside the United States. Other countries will not recognize wills made here and vice versa.

Essential Phrases Needed in Your Will

Although it is true that a will is most often not contested, you still need to be sure that the wording cannot be mistaken. Again, it is recommended that you seek legal help in your estate planning so that many of these potential pitfalls can be avoided.

One simple clause that needs to be in your will pertains to what happens when a specific item is no longer available to be distributed to a particular beneficiary, even though it is promised to a specified person in your will. After all, once the will is written, you may choose to sell that item, or someone else may take it, making it unavailable. A question can be brought up in this case as to whether another item of similar value, or cash, needs to be taken out of the estate to make up for it.

If the item is not of much value, then it probably will not be a concern. The relative would probably simply let it go. If, however, the item had considerable value to it, there is reason to expect the relative to want his or her promised share. You can simply add a little phrase to take care of this problem. For example, "If [the item] is in my possession at the time of my death…." The wording here gives no promise of anything else if it is not in your possession at the time of death, so nothing else will be expected.

Another situation can occur relating to the time of death: if both the husband and the wife die at the same time. If both have separate wills, it can be a matter of concern, especially in cases of former marriages and children from those marriages.

For instance, problems may occur if both have children from a former marriage and both die together. Suppose that the husband willed his possessions to his wife if he should die first. He plans to sustain a surviving spouse, but leaves his possessions to his son if he and his wife died at the same time. It is possible that they could be in a car accident together and that the wife might outlive the husband by five days. In this situation, the man's son would get nothing, his wife would get everything, and her will would then pass it all to her children.

One little phrase could be added to remedy this kind of situation. For example, you could add a clause such as, "If my wife survives me more than 40 days, then…" It is clear that she would need the support if she outlives him. A second part may also be added: "If we die at the same time, or if it cannot be determined who died last, then let my son be named as the beneficiary." This way an alternate beneficiary is named, which prevents the money from bypassing the son in a case where husband and wife die at about the same time.

One other clause that you will need in your will deals with everything else that has not yet been mentioned. It offers a way to put those things in — even things that you may have forgotten about. It needs to be worded similarly to, "I leave the remainder of my estate to…." Without this simple clause, there could be grounds for the remainder of your assets to be divided up according to state rules.

Place Your Will Where It Can Be Found

It is very important that your survivors know where they can find your will. In many states, it is necessary that the original document be used to settle the estate. If it cannot be located, then it is discounted, and your estate will be treated as if there were no will at all.

In some cases, this can be overcome by proving that you had intent to create a will. Obviously, though, it will not always be successful and could cost a good deal of money trying to prove it.

13
An Overview of Trusts

Trusts are the most common way to put your assets outside the probate system, and there is plenty of room for variation to make sure one fits your specific needs. A trust may not be for everyone, but they do have many uses when you have a vision for passing your legacy on to your heirs. Here are some details about this form of estate planning.

Definition of a Trust

A trust is a legal entity created with the assets of a grantor but managed by a designated person who oversees them for one or more people. The trustee is appointed by the grantor and could consist of one or more persons (trustees) entrusted with the task. A trustee may also be an agency, such as a trust company or bank chosen to manage the affairs of the trust estate. Although the assets are technically the property of the trustees, it is their duty to manage the assets for the benefit of the heirs. Generally, the trustees are not allowed to touch the assets for their own use except for fees. When there is a written document, it will be in the form of a deed.

Forming a Trust

A trust can be formed by four different means, although this may vary with your location. Here are the four ways a trust can be established:

- A written document

- A will

- A court order

- An oral declaration

A trust must also have certain details laid out in order to have validity. There are three details that must be clear and specific. The first is that there needs to be a clear intent to create a trust. A second detail that must be fulfilled is that the assets that are to be placed in the trust must be spelled out. Some types of items may require a written trust deed before they can be put into it, and this could vary with your location. Third, beneficiaries are to be named. In some cases, a class of beneficiaries can be named, and then the trustees may decide the precise beneficiary based on those terms established by the grantor.

In some places, it is also possible to create a trust, be the trustee, and also be the beneficiary at the same time. This is generally called a revocable trust, but it needs to be set up carefully to ensure it is legal.

The Purposes of a Trust

Creating a trust can produce several benefits, both for those who are creating the trust and for those who will be the beneficiaries. The primary purposes of the trust are to:

- Remove the assets from the possibility of estate taxes and probate

- Place assets into the hands of loved ones faster than the probate system would allow

- Place controls on the expenditures of the assets

- Enable assets to survive to the benefit of future generations

- Protect assets from creditors

- Hold assets for minors until they are older

- Provide privacy — wills are usually public, but trust assets are private

Other purposes exist, but these are among the most common, and other categories will loosely fit into one of these.

Provisions of a Trust

As has already been mentioned, a trust can provide you with many options for determining what happens to your assets. Each of the following aspects or details of a trust are provided below so that you can see what possible options you may have when you set up a trust.

The People

This part includes the names of each of those involved:

- The grantor

- The trustees

- The beneficiaries

The Assets

This part of the trust will need to specify what assets are under the control of the trust and the trustees.

The Conditions

Any specifications to govern the assets are laid out and decided upon. This will partly depend on the type of trust it is and the reason for its creation. This is where you can set forth your vision for the control of your assets for many years into the future. Everything you want done with the assets, however, needs to be spelled out as carefully and as clearly as possible.

An example of what can be accomplished would be if you have a son or daughter who has poor spending habits, and you want to prevent the money from being wasted. You can establish, for instance, that an allowance be given to him or her every so often. You may make exceptions, such as for the purpose of education or medical needs, and maybe some other needs, until he or she turns a certain age.

In other cases, you may provide the use of a house, which will then pass on to his or her heirs when the time comes. This keeps the asset out of the control of the son or daughter and merely enables them to "use" those assets.

The Types of Trusts

The type of trust you choose will be determined largely by what you want to accomplish. For instance, a dynasty trust is an excellent tool when you want to skip generations for tax purposes, which will enable your estate to escape many taxes and be able to survive with a much larger portion than it could otherwise.

This section will simply provide a quick overview of many types of trusts so that you can see the various overall purposes when compared to each other. This should enable you to select one that will be the most beneficial to your needs. More details will be provided in following sections.

Simple Trust

This is the most common type. A simple trust is one that places certain assets under the control of a trustee until an appointed time. At that time, the trustee will turn over all assets in the trust to the beneficiary. This type of trust can be used if the child is a minor or if the money is to be held until the individual matures enough to know how to responsibly handle the assets given.

Bypass Trust

This kind of trust is designed to hold assets above the allowable tax-free amounts to avoid paying estate taxes on it. In 2007, this amount was $2 million per individual or $4 million per married couple. In 2009, this amount will be raised to $3.5 million per individual and become unlimited in 2010.

Charitable Trust

This trust is established for purposes of giving assets to a charity. This needs to be set up carefully and can go on indefinitely. It offers many benefits to the creator.

Dynasty Trust

This trust is also called a generation-skipping trust. It is designed to avoid estate taxes and to pass the assets down to the third generation or further. It bypasses estate taxes when assets are placed into the trust for the grandchildren.

Irrevocable Trust

This type of trust cannot be changed or eliminated once it has been created — not by the creator or anyone else. The only thing that can happen is that it be administered as written in its documents. Unless very careful thought is given to it beforehand, this kind of trust can create trouble, simply because the future is unpredictable.

Living Trust

A living trust is also called an "inter vivos" trust and is simply one that is created while you are still alive. The grantor remains the trustee over assets in the living trust while still alive. Depending on the type of living trust you choose, it may enable you to escape estate taxes and probate.

Life Insurance Trust

This is usually created before death and is then used for deposit of the proceeds from a life insurance policy. This basically creates the estate.

QTIP Trust

This trust, which stands for "qualified terminable interest property trust," enables you to make a trust out of property that would otherwise be disqualified. It can be used to place property that is above the personal exemption level and yet still be controlled by the trust terms. It is not exempt from estate taxes, however.

Revocable Living Trust

This kind of trust allows the trustor to be able to control and use the assets of the trust for his or her own purposes. The trustor is able to add or subtract assets from the trust, change the terms and administration, and cancel it altogether if desired. It can also be changed into an irrevocable trust at any time. This kind of trust offers limited legal protection of assets placed in it, because technically you are still the owner.

Secret Trust

This kind of trust can be given when there are beneficiaries that need to remain unknown. While these are rare, they permit the trustor to give assets to an unknown person or organization. These have been used to support a mistress or illegitimate children, but may also have other purposes.

Spendthrift Trust

This trust can be created by a trustor or by an individual for his or her own purposes. It is designed to control assets for an individual who has difficulty handling his or her own money or assets.

Testamentary Trust

This type of trust is created from the will. The assets are specified in the will, as are all other terms and appointments.

A More Detailed View of Trusts

Simple Trust

The most common type of trust is called a simple trust. Trust terms can overlap some, which means that there may also be some other names that refer to the same thing. Basically, any trust is either simple or complex.

Three things can define a simple trust:

- Distributes all income (interest) each year it is received

- Does not require distribution of the principal (in that year)

- Does not have any charitable beneficiary

A trust can vary between a simple and a complex form in any two consecutive years. It is based on the terms and conditions that are set forth when it was created. Also, it cannot be a grantor trust or one that the grantor has control of. An example of this would be a trust designated to give the heir a portion of the trust assets when he turns 21. In the 20th year of his life, he may receive some interest from the trust, which qualifies it as simple; but in the following year, the 21st, he will receive some of the principle, which makes it complex.

An exception to this is the trust that allows the trustees to decide to distribute or accumulate the interest or where the beneficiaries decide it. If there is an option about the distributions, it is a complex trust. All trusts are complex in their final year because principal is distributed.

Bypass Trust

Bypass trusts are a common tool designed to escape a double inheritance tax. This would normally occur when either a husband or a wife dies and the estate passes to the surviving spouse. Since estate tax is due upon death, there is a tax. Then, after the remaining spouse dies, there is again another tax taken out of the estate. Since each one is given a personal exemption of $2 million for 2008, and then $3.5 million in 2009, this is most beneficial to those making more than that in income.

A bypass trust is designed to enable the estate to be passed to the children and taxed only once, taking full advantage of the personal estate tax exemption. This can happen when all the assets of the first spouse to die are placed in a bypass trust. Under the terms of this trust, these assets:

- Are placed in an irrevocable trust

- Are given limited use by the surviving spouse

- Make the children the beneficiaries

- Cannot be directed to different beneficiaries

- Escape estate taxes until the surviving spouse dies

Besides being designed to bypass the double taxes that would occur otherwise, this estate is also intended to make sure the right beneficiaries receive the inheritance they should. Otherwise, when the assets of the first to die are passed to the other mate, the remaining mate could completely alter the beneficiaries, and the loved ones of the first spouse might not receive anything.

This trust ensures that the intended beneficiaries receive the assets intended for them. This is especially good when there is a remarriage and more than one set of children.

Charitable Trust

A charitable trust, or charitable remainder trust (CRT), is a great way to save some money on estate taxes and still be able to give to your favorite charity. By creating this kind of trust, which is irrevocable, you reduce your tax liability, can still draw some income from the trust, and reduce your taxes by any amount given to the charity.

Even though a charitable trust is irrevocable, you can set it up in such a way that:

- You are the trustee

- You can change the beneficiary

- You receive an income for yourself and your spouse

- You have some control over the assets, possibly to invest

The income you receive is an amount of your choosing. It continues, if you set it up that way, to provide an income for your surviving spouse as well. Upon the death of the remaining spouse, all assets of the trust are then given to the charity.

Another good benefit of the CRT is that you can use it for those assets that are highly appreciated but can generate little income. If you sell it, you would lose up to about 15 percent of its value from capital gains. By placing it in the trust, however, you can keep its value and pass the savings on to its designated beneficiaries.

All income from a charity trust is taxable as income. This would be any amount of the assets you receive as a designated income for yourself and your spouse. Anything placed in the trust escapes estate taxes and is tax deductible.

The IRS does require that at least 5 percent of the trust be given each year to the beneficiary. Any less than this and the trust may be disqualified as a means to escape estate taxes. For best results, it is suggested that no more than 10 percent be given each year.

Charitable Lead Trusts and Charitable Remainder Trusts

A Charitable Lead Trust (CLT) and a CRT are very similar. They both provide the same tax benefits and the same degree of control over the assets while you are alive, and both have the power to deliver your assets where you want, both while you live and after you pass away.

Instead of you having payments made to your named beneficiaries while you are alive, as with a CRT, and then the charity receiving the balance, a CLT works the opposite way. The charity now receives payments during your lifetime. When you pass away, then your beneficiaries receive the balance of the trust.

The same tax benefits are still in place as with a CRT. The only difference is the recipients of the assets.

There are two kinds of CLTs: the grantor lead trust and the nongrantor lead trust. Both of these can be made either for a designated number of years or for the length of your life or someone else's (your spouse's, for instance) life.

A grantor lead trust is where you place the assets into a trust, and then the trust distributes the designated payments to the charity or organization of your choice. The unique feature, however, is that the while the grantor enjoys the tax benefits of the trust, the grantor also pays the taxes on all money given to the charity.

A nongrantor lead trust, which is the more popular of the two types, enables you to have some tax benefits. Any growth taking place in the trust is passed on to the charity — along with the taxes — giving you the tax reduction you want and still enabling you to contribute to charitable causes.

Defective Grantor Trust

In spite of its name, which makes it sound inadequate, this is actually a very effective tool for reducing taxes on your estate — income taxes, that is. The "defective" part simply means that not everything that applies to a trust actually applies in this case. The result is that you get a tax break. Here is how this strategy works.

A defective trust requires that assets be placed into an irrevocable trust, which also means that the grantor cannot retain any control over any of the assets. There is, however, one stipulation that also must apply: The income is given to the grantor, but the grantor cannot be the beneficiary.

Another stipulation that applies is that the grantor has the right to replace the property with property or assets of equal value. What happens, as far as estate taxes are concerned, is that by buying the property in the trust at fair market value and receiving the income from it, the grantor has purchased the property from himself. This means that there is no profit and no gift transfer takes place.

Income from the property continues to come in, and the grantor pays the income taxes on it. This removes future appreciation from it, and it can also receive a stepped-up basis (current value) at death.

Disclaimer Trusts

A disclaimer trust is a unique way to avoid having to add the particular assets of the deceased spouse to an existing account of the surviving spouse. This allows for various tax breaks and savings of a larger portion of the estate. It offers the assets of the spouse to the surviving spouse, who then will refuse to accept those assets so that they will be transferred automatically to a predesignated trust. The best feature is that it enables the surviving spouse to use up the spouse's tax deduction so that he or she does not need to pay taxes at death.

Like most other things that are done this way, it has to follow precise steps in order to work as intended. Several things must happen in order. For this reason, it is necessary to use an estate planner to be sure it is set up correctly. Among them are:

- The estate must be "offered" to the surviving spouse

- Portions to pass into the trust must be disclaimed entirely, with no asset removed

- It must be predirected to the intended trust by the deceased

- Special terms of the trust must be carefully outlined

- The surviving spouse cannot have testamentary powers

Besides the tax benefits that are applied when the proper portion of the estate is "disclaimed," the necessary added incentive for the spouse to disclaim it is that the gain from the trust goes to the surviving spouse. This provides an income for the spouse while he or she is alive, and then the children inherit it later.

The spouse can serve as the trustee of the trust, but cannot have any power to appoint one. Nor can the surviving spouse have any control over the assets other than what has been previously determined in the deceased spouse's will.

The only way that this can work is if it is planned with both spouses being fully aware of what to do and what not to do. It can be rather tricky. If the surviving spouse makes a wrong move, the assets will be transferred to his or her estate and taxes will be due.

CASE STUDY: GIDEON ROTHSCHILD ESQ.

Gideon Rothschild Esq.
Moses & Singer LLP
405 Lexington Ave.
New York, NY 10174
Tel: 212-554-7806
Fax: 917-206-4306
http://www.mosessinger.com

Estate planning is all about keeping more of your money and being able to pass it on to your heirs. The choice is rather simple when it comes to your estate and taxes. Proper estate planning allows you to remain in control of your assets — and not the taxman, allowing you to pass more of your assets on to your heirs.

Here in New York, we help people to save a lot of money by working around the tax laws. Besides federal taxes, there are also state estate taxes that you have to pay. People have to take that into account, too.

CASE STUDY: GIDEON ROTHSCHILD ESQ.

To give you an example, take the couple that has a $4 million estate, with the husband having $3.5 million, and the wife having the remaining half-million dollars. While most people prepare for the federal taxes, this couple, if they do not have an estate plan that takes this into consideration, would still lose about $250,000 in state taxes after they die. This is unnecessary and could easily be avoided.

One solution to this situation would be if the husband were to put $1 million into a trust. This would leave the wife, assuming she is the last to die, with $3 million. If she died in 2009, when the personal tax exemption is $3.5 million, she would not pay any taxes.

Another popular option in recent years is the disclaimer trust. At the death of the husband (or, first to die) the money is left to the spouse, but there are also specific instructions in the will that give her the option to reject the inheritance (or a portion of it) if she wants. She has up to 9 months to make that decision, and this also gives her some time to heal emotionally so that the best decision can be made. The will also directs the assets or money that she rejects to be placed into a credit shelter trust, which would give the estate asset protection from creditors because the assets are never in her name. If enough money is left to her, she would not even have a maintenance income, either. This adds further protection and really is unnecessary in this case.

Another great option would be to give her a "unitrust interest."

That simply means she gets a fixed percentage (typically between 3 and 5 percent, depending on state law) of the value of the trust determined annually. Of course, if she needs more than that amount, the trustee can be given discretion to distribute principal to her. The main advantage of this approach is that the trustee can invest the trust assets in a diversified portfolio of stocks and bonds without sacrificing the spouse's interest or the remainder beneficiary's desire for capital appreciation. A unitrust is particularly beneficial where there is a spouse and children from a prior marriage, since it avoids the typical conflict that arises with standard form trusts.

Estate planning has some great challenges coming up in the next few years, partly due to Congressional decisions that will need to be made in 2010, and other new areas that have recently come over the horizon — due to modern reproductive technology and children born through artificial conceptions — beyond death of the biological parent. Changes will probably be coming soon, and it is important to keep your estate plan up to date and on top of developments and new laws as they occur.

Dynasty Trust

A dynasty trust has the ability to pass your inheritance on to your grandchildren and to escape estate taxes by doing so. This trust, which is also referred to as a generation-skipping trust, makes your grandchildren the beneficiaries of your estate. In some states, however, a dynasty trust can now be continued indefinitely, or for up to 1,000 years. The advantage here, however, is that you do not have to be a resident of a state in order to create a trust in it.

Typical estate taxes will greatly reduce the estate each time the taxes are applied. This, of course, happens every time someone dies. Between the grandparents and the grandchildren, this means that taxes are taken out twice, which reduces the taxable estate by at least 45 percent each time. The heirs, then, are given only a piece of the original estate, and the government receives a large portion of it.

A dynasty trust enables the heirs to receive a much larger portion by bypassing the tax process once. Although it will do nothing to help the grantor escape taxes, the next generation, the children, will benefit the most.

A dynasty trust gives the creator of the trust a great deal of control even after he or she is gone. Relatives, children, or even spouses can be excluded from a dynasty trust. This helps you retain control of your assets for generations to come.

This kind of trust can be created in an open-ended way, allowing you to add assets when you are ready to do so. You can, however, still enjoy the assets for a time and then, at your death, they pass on to the control of the designated trustee or trustees. This enables your children to enjoy the use of the assets as you designated.

Placing your assets into a dynasty trust is probably the best way to ensure that your vision will last long into the future. Since the time could extend considerably beyond the lifetime of your great-grandchildren, it is a great tool for enabling you to influence generations to come.

One problem, however, is that you need to build into the terms of the dynasty trust some way for future trustees to slightly alter it. This is necessary because you have no idea what kind of life people living five generations from now will face. Terms and conditions you set forth may not even apply at that time or may be impossible to fulfill. For instance, what if all undergraduate and graduate education in the future is done on computers at home? Who knows what things like virtual reality will bring to our doorstep? Imagine, if you can, the reverse situation. How could someone from the late 1700s determine how to distribute your inheritance today, and would you appreciate the controls they set forth as conditions for you?

It is necessary, with the help of an experienced estate planner, to create a dynasty trust that has flexibility built in. The document needs to be rather detailed but must still allow for changes to meet future needs.

Irrevocable Trust

An irrevocable trust is just what it says — irrevocable. Once it is in place there can be no going back, no matter how determined you are or how serious the mistake. For that reason, you would need to give some serious thought as to why you would ever need to create such a trust.

There are, however, some occasions in which it could come in handy. One of these is if you think there will be an attempt to change the terms in the trust by some less-than-honest children, an ex-spouse, or other relatives. This does happen, and the larger the estate, the more useful this type of trust could become.

The problem, however, occurs in the realm of the unexpected. While you may will your assets to your spouse in an irrevocable will, you cannot see what the future will bring. For instance, you could die shortly after your create the irrevocable trust and then the assets pass to your spouse. There could be a remarriage and then all assets would pass to whomever the spouse wanted. Any children you have would become upset and may try to sue for an adjustment of the terms of the trust, or have it thrown out altogether.

Other situations may occur if you try to leave all your assets to your children and leave out the spouse, who may already have plenty. However, state law in some places demands that the spouse get at least a specified amount. This could cause the trust arrangements to be thrown out altogether if it were taken to court. Irrevocable trusts need to be very carefully thought out and not rushed into, because not even the creator of an irrevocable trust can change it once it is established.

Still, irrevocable trusts are commonly used to satisfy the IRS requirements of an Irrevocable Life Insurance Trust (ILIT). This trust must be established at least three years before the death of the grantor, and there cannot be any control of the assets by the grantor during that time. Upon the death of the grantor, the insurance proceeds are placed into the trust. If these strict qualifications are not met according to the IRS, the tax benefits will be immediately removed.

Living Trust

A living trust gives you the power to be able to put your assets beyond the realm of probate and still allows you to have some control over them. As its name implies, it is useful while you are still alive, but will also place your assets into the future reach of those who you want to have them.

This type of trust, which is also called an inter vivos trust, a revocable trust, or a frantor trust, has many uses. One of the most popular is that you can name yourself as the trustee, which gives you the power to use your assets as desired. These may also be irrevocable living trusts. Other benefits are:

- Assets in a trust do not go through probate, which provides much quicker access to them

- You can name a secondary trustee in the event you become unable to manage your assets

- You can name secondary beneficiaries, who will receive the assets after you are gone

- You choose the terms and conditions for the use of the assets that the trustee must fulfill

- It places all your assets in the trust outside of probate, which could be as much as 10 percent of the assets

One negative aspect of a living trust, however, is that it does not take the assets out of the reach of estate taxes. So, while it will save you money in one way, you pay for it in another. Since estate taxes must be paid within nine months of the death of the trustor, it is absolutely necessary that you have separate funds available for this expense, as well as any maintenance costs for the spouse and funeral expenses.

Joint living trusts can also be created. This gives power for the husband

and the wife to have property rights within the single trust. Their assets are kept separate, they retain control, and they are also able to choose their own beneficiaries. You each also retain the right to add or subtract assets from the trust, since you each appoint yourselves as the initial trustees over your own half of the account. Each spouse also has the right to terminate the trust at will, in which case the property goes back to the original owner.

Problems may arise in a joint living trust if there is property contained in it that is jointly owned. About the only way this can be resolved is to have two new deeds to half of the property be made and then entered into the trust in that form.

When combined with a pourover will, this is an excellent way to have the coverage you need for your estate. A pourover will causes all your assets not mentioned in the will, or already in another instrument, to be placed into your trust when you die. Then, because you have already named your beneficiaries, all your assets will go where you have designated them.

When you are talking with your estate planner about your needs in creating the living trust, be sure to find out whether you are in a community property state. If you are, you will be required to leave a portion of your assets to the surviving spouse, which could be as much as a half of the estate. If you do not, and it becomes challenged, the court will rewrite your will and distribute according to law. Children also have a right to a percentage as well. Find out what those percentages are where you live before you make your choices. If you move out of that state, you will want to see an estate planning attorney in order to readjust your trusts and wills accordingly.

Another benefit of having a living trust in place is that it provides security should you become unable to manage your estate on your own. Since you have already named a secondary beneficiary for your trust, that person would handle your trust assets according to the directions of the trust.

Life Insurance Trust

A life insurance trust enables you to place life insurance proceeds outside of probate.

This gives you much faster access to the funds and saves you from having to pay probate costs. However, it has a number of strict regulations placed on it by the IRS, which must be met, or your proceeds will be counted as part of your estate and will then have to go through probate.

When properly planned, though, a life insurance trust, commonly called an Irrevocable Life Insurance Trust (ILIT) can save you a good deal of money. Like any trust, the assets from the policy are immediately placed outside your estate, enabling it to avoid the heavy estate taxes.

Being that it is outside your estate and that the heirs can rather quickly receive the proceeds from it, this trust places cash at their disposal almost immediately. This may be necessary if cash is needed to close some loose ends in the estate, such as buying back stock, paying estate taxes, providing for survivor maintenance, closing business interests, or finishing real estate transactions.

With an ILIT, careful planning is needed in order to make sure it fulfills the requirements of the IRS. Here are some of those requirements:

- The trust must be created first, at least three years prior to the grantor's death

- The trust must then be funded with money for the premiums

- The trust must buy the policy

- The grantor cannot have any control over the trust

- The proceeds must be placed into the trust

In a situation in which you may want to transfer an existing life insurance policy to the life insurance trust, you will need to create the ILIT first. Then, you simply make the transfer. Be sure, however, to follow any steps that a qualified estate planner may direct. This is because he or she is familiar with the changing IRS requirements that must be met in order for the proceeds to be tax exempt. In recent years, the IRS has been looking for any slight fault so that the full estate taxes can be paid.

With an ILIT, there is a potential problem that you need to be aware of. Whenever assets are placed into an ILIT, they are not normally tax exempt. The only way to make them so is to provide a "present interest" to the heirs. A document known as a Crummey Letter (from a 1968 court case involving Clifford Crummey) will allow this problem to be overcome. This letter must be sent to each potential beneficiary of the insurance trust to let them know that funds are now available. You will need to tell each of them in advance that the money is needed to pay for the insurance premiums. Otherwise, they are legitimately able to withdraw those funds.

When you consider which type of life insurance policy to buy, you can save the most with a whole life policy. This may surprise some since it is true that you can buy more insurance per dollar with term insurance. However, a whole life policy becomes self-sustaining with cash values after a while. When that happens, you will no longer need to fund the trust; it will take care of itself.

One consideration that you should be aware of is your own insurability. Since you cannot buy the insurance in advance of setting up the trust, you may not know whether you can buy it at all, or what the cost will be. They still must be done simultaneously. Be careful not to let the cost of your premiums take away your personal tax exemption.

Also, keep in mind that it is an irrevocable trust. After it has been established, you have no power to change anything in it. Choose your beneficiaries carefully, and be aware that an "amendor" clause will allow a trustee to make some changes.

Pet Trusts

If you want to ensure that your pet has all the care that it will need during its remaining years, you can do so with a pet trust. All you need to do is name a trustee who will handle the funds and then place funds into the account.

The trust will need to be funded with enough to last for the expected lifespan of your pet, as well as enough to ensure that the potential health needs of the pet are also met. You need to designate just how much of the funds can be withdrawn each week or month for food, clothes, entertainment, and education, as well as making sure that there is enough to pay for maintenance costs of the trust. Be careful about putting too much into the trust, as this could provide legal grounds for the trust to be denied.

A caregiver of your pet should be named, as well as an alternate in case someone changes his or her mind. It may not be a bad idea to have the pet given a microchip for ID purposes. Some people have continued receiving money from pet trusts simply by replacing the animal with another after the pet died.

Pet trusts are currently only legal in about one-third of the states, but others may be in the process of allowing them. If your state does not have one yet, you may need to provide for your pet using another method. Taxes on pet trusts are also different than other trusts, so you should be aware of what methods are used before establishing one.

The Qualified Domestic Trust (QDOT)

The Qualified Domestic Trust (QDOT) is for spouses who are not American citizens. Tax laws place limits on the amount that can be transferred tax free to spouses who are not citizens of the United States. It appears that there is a fear that too much money will be removed from the country.

In 1988, laws were passed that put a limit on what had previously been an unlimited marital tax exemption. These laws concerned the size of gifts that could be passed from one spouse to a noncitizen spouse upon the death of the U.S. citizen. This new law limits that amount to $100,000. Further laws are now being worked on in relation to certain countries where this law has been adjusted to favor the citizens of those countries. Canada is one of them, and the law applies only to Canadian citizens who are currently living in the United States.

In addition to this restriction of limited gifts, the noncitizen spouse should not serve as the trustee of the account for other maximum tax advantages. Of course, you never know which spouse will die first, so you may want to have a corporation serve as trustee. There is no problem concerning taxes if the non-U.S. citizen should die first. The rest of the QDOT trust is like that of a QTIP.

One way around some of these tax problems is for part of your estate to pass to your spouse directly upon your death. Include in it the option that gives your spouse the right to refuse the outright gift and allow it to pass into a QDOT of his or her own making. He or she has up to nine months to do this. During that time, the noncitizen spouse could seek to become a citizen, or hope that Congress may make changes to this law.

Qualified Terminable Interest Property (QTIP) Trust

This trust will enable married couples to have several advantages. A QTIP trust provides a way around some of the normal difficulties that may be experienced, especially for those who are married for the second time with previous children.

A QTIP Trust allows the married couple to take full advantage of the combined personal exemption, provide for the surviving spouse, reduce taxes, and still enable the descendants of the first deceased to pass on his or her inheritance according to his or her wishes.

One of the qualifications of a QTIP is that all the income from the trust must be given to the surviving spouse. So, if the assets of the trust are in the form of stocks, bonds, mutual funds, and other forms, the surviving spouse will receive sustenance from those assets while alive. Also, if there are any terms that allow any of the principal to be passed to the survivor, then this will be done through the appointed trustee.

The assets placed into the trust are those that are above the personal exemption of the deceased. The remainder, then, which is placed in the trust, avoids all taxes until the survivor passes on. At that time, the remaining assets of the trust will go entirely to the beneficiary that was named by the first married partner to die.

More of this will be discussed in Chapter 14, which is especially devoted to QTIPs.

Spendthrift Trust

A spendthrift trust is usually created in order to protect the assets of a trust in some way. The most common purpose is when there is a beneficiary who is unable to spend responsibly.

A spendthrift trust does not necessarily need to have the words "spendthrift trust" in it to be designated as such. The purpose will still be there and the means to control spendthrift spending will also be there, in the wording of the trust document. The way it works is that the ability to determine the use of the assets is not placed into the hands of the beneficiary. Rather, the control lies with the trustee, who is responsible for ensuring that the assets are not misused or spent foolishly.

A spendthrift trust is also usually an irrevocable one, so that the clause cannot be removed or the purpose of protection changed. This kind of trust is also one in which there are special clauses that prevent creditors from getting control of the assets in the trust. This can be accomplished by denying claims for assets that are greater than the payments that the beneficiary receives. A trustee can also make direct payments to creditors.

A spendthrift clause may have other functions, too. Since a spendthrift trust is irrevocable, this allows the terms to be untouchable in case spouses or children want to gain access to the principal. For a young lady who keeps getting married, this prevents her or one of her husbands from touching the funds.

For children who have no real understanding of the value of money, this is the kind of trust you want to establish. The money will be there, it will last a long time, and some may even be saved for the grandchildren.

Another use of spendthrift trusts is for a person who realizes his or her irresponsible spending habits. Generally, a friend or relative may offer this tip and encourage them to place their own assets under such control. By doing this, they place their assets under the oversight of a trustee, and that trustee has the right to say "no" when needed.

This type of trust, however, is not permitted in many places. Because this type of trust could enable someone to get deep into debt irresponsibly and then place it in such a trust to avoid payments, many locations have outlawed it. If you are interested in a spendthrift trust, you would have to see an estate planner about the terms and the possibility of creating one.

There is also the possibility that a spendthrift clause could be added to another type of trust, such as a QTIP or bypass trust. If one or more of your children or grandchildren, or their spouses, have much debt, this would allow you to help them with regular distributions and still prevent creditors from getting access to the trust. While it helps their situation, a spouse cannot alter the size of the distribution or seize the principal. Thus, their children can still receive an inheritance as well.

Testamentary Trust

A testamentary trust is one created through a will — a person's last testament. The word trust does not need to be used, but the intent of a will may be enough to indicate that a trust is either intended or may be necessary to carry out the expressed will of the deceased. In either case, a trust that results from a will carries specific privileges for the assets that are to be placed in the trust.

Testamentary trusts are often created for children until they are old enough to receive the benefits. In some states, a child can receive the full trust assets at age 18. These days, however, it is better to provide the terms of a trust in a will rather than leave it to speculation as to how the assets can best be protected until the children are mature enough to receive them. It is necessary to name the grantor (the person who is giving the assets; in this case, the deceased), the beneficiaries, and the trustee, which could be the executor of the will. It is also a good idea to mention how the assets are to be distributed.

Although this is all that is needed for a trust to be created, it is better to sit down with an estate planner and work out some details. This way, it may be possible to save a larger portion of the assets, and a wiser provision, preservation, and distribution of the assets can be made, too. More than one trust can be created from a single will.

Creating a testamentary trust rather than another trust form will cause some potential benefits to be lost, but there still are some benefits available. One of them is that taxes paid on the trust itself, rather than after the beneficiary gets the assets, will receive a much better tax rate. There could be savings of thousands of dollars in a brief time period.

There are many potential uses of a testamentary trust. For example, you could turn a living trust into a charitable trust by designating it as such in your will. The terms would also need to be specified. This would enable you to leave a regular income to your children or spouse, make regular donations to your favorite charity, and then have the remainder of the trust be given to that charity upon the death of the beneficiary.

Many kinds of trusts can be created from a will, but careful planning is needed. For instance, you could also create a dynasty trust or a spendthrift trust.

However, the best way to avoid probate and some of the estate taxes is to create the trust while you are still living. Once the assets are funded into the trust, this enables you to reduce those taxes by the assets in the trust. Assets placed into a trust through your will are subject to go through probate. This means that those assets could be tied up for three years. If you plan on using a testamentary trust, be sure you have other assets that will enable you to pay estate taxes within the first nine months after your demise. There should also be enough to provide adequate maintenance (if needed) for the spouse, as well as funeral expenses.

Unitrusts

Many states are now allowing a trust called a unitrust. Some states do not yet permit it. Where it is allowed, however, there may be the option for the trustee to change the way the trust is administered if the original documents of the trust permit it. The justification for the change must be that it would make it easier for the trustee to fulfill the intentions of the grantor.

One of the major reasons for doing this is that it could give the trustee greater liberty to distribute the assets more easily — and as needed. This would mean that where a larger amount is needed by the beneficiary, a larger amount could be given. The opposite is also true, however, since distributions are not necessarily mandatory.

Unitrusts can be designed with many options and are often associated with charitable remainder trusts, but do not have to be. Different agencies that use them may have many different names for them.

A unitrust could be set up so that the distributions are based on the actual income that the trust has. When it does not perform so well, the distributions are less. This is an excellent situation for when the principal needs to be protected so that it can be given intact to the charitable organization or another beneficiary. The amount to be paid out is recalculated each year. In some cases, there is an allowable option to "make up" for smaller distributions when there is a larger income than has been designated.

Other situations in unitrusts allow for a fixed percentage to be disbursed, even if it must be paid out of the principal. Unitrusts are often made for a set period of time, such as up to 20 years, or possibly for the life of the grantor and the surviving spouse.

Offshore Trusts

This is now, more than ever, an option to use in your estate planning. Many of the offshore trusts are very similar to what is available here in the United States, but may offer you even better protection. You may want to consider using one for your plans.

While considering this form of asset protection, use a reputable estate planner who is aware of the ins and outs of offshore estate planning. One of the key elements to understand is that it is not a way to hide your assets from the IRS. Rather, the best estate planning is sure to report to the IRS any income and any other reporting as required by law. You do not want to be found guilty of noncompliance with the tax laws; this would surely lead to trouble. You can also be sure that they will carefully look at any offshore trusts and other dealings that you have out of the country.

Offshore trusts and other instruments are especially valuable when you have beneficiaries who are likely to have creditors come calling on them. Perhaps you feel that they may be debt prone, and one day it may catch up to them, even if they are not in debt now. You can help preserve their inheritance by using offshore instruments, such as:

- Foreign Asset Protection Trusts (FAPT)

- Foreign limited liability companies

- Offshore unitrusts

- Offshore mutual funds

- International trading companies

- Swiss annuities

- Foreign stock trading accounts

- Registered foreign sales facilities

- Foreign security trusts

- Foreign bank accounts

- And a few more

These instruments are especially valuable to estate planning because judgments that are valid in the U.S. have no meaning in foreign countries. These lawsuits simply are not recognized unless the court proceedings are again initiated in that country. Besides that, other countries require that lawyers pay for the court costs up front, and if they lose the case, then they must cover the client's cost as well. This makes it unlikely that creditors will come after assets held overseas, unless they have good proof and plenty of money to gain from it.

You need to be extra careful about whom you hire to help you with offshore investments. There are scams out there that operate with the policy of simply not reporting your assets to where you should. This is illegal. To protect yourself, even if you believe an agency to be reputable, check with other agencies to make sure you know about all required reporting and to whom you must report. You will not want to take any unnecessary chances with not reporting — this could be considered hiding assets for tax evasion purposes.

Insurance Trusts for Children

Buying life insurance is a great way to provide for children if anything should ever happen to their parents. An insurance policy can also be used to create a trust and provide for the children's support, medical expenses, and education, and leave them with some additional funds.

Insurance can be used to set up a trust for children and help them receive assets as needed. If you choose to name children as beneficiaries, you can also specify what percentage each of them is to receive.

Another way that could make things a little easier, though, would be to name a trustee on the policy and state that the money is to be used for the children. Be sure to select someone you trust; you also may want to name only one, instead of a husband and wife. With divorces as rampant as they are, naming both may not be a good idea.

Several other options are also available, such as having the insurance proceeds put into a Uniform Transfers to Minors Act (UTMA) plan for your state, a child's trust, or a pot trust. The simplest form would be the UTMA, since no formal procedure needs to be followed; simply go down to your bank to create it. This is one form that is almost the same in every state, and it exists for education purposes. Only a limited amount, however, can be placed into an UTMA at one time.

Child's Trust

This is one way to control the assets of your estate for the benefit of your children. It is unique in that it allows you to dictate the age at which your children can receive their remaining inheritance. Other forms of trusts for children are dictated by the state and are generally disbursed at either age 18, 21, or 25. In many cases, especially if the amount being given to each child is large, this usually is not a good idea.

A child's trust gives the trustee a rather liberal use of the assets for the needs of the beneficiaries. The assets can be used for their support, health, maintenance, and education. Portions can be given for their education as needed, and it can also be used as needed. For instance, if one child has a great medical need, then this need could easily be met.

Preservation of the assets until the child becomes a mature adult is the goal with a child's trust. You can set the age at 35, or any age that you think is good. Parents also have the option to stagger the payments in order to enable the assets to last longer. A possibility is to give one-third of the estate each at ages 25, 30, and 35. By doing so, you may limit their ability to use large quantities and help them to plan by letting them know when future portions will come.

Family Pot Trusts

Making sure your children are taken care if you should die earlier than expected is important. It is not that difficult and can easily be provided for in your will. A family pot trust may be just the instrument you are looking for to accomplish this goal. The following details some of its features.

A pot trust is generally one trust that is created for all of your children. If they are widely spread apart in age, however, you may want to create one for the older children and one for the younger. If the older children are young adults, then you can give them their portion of the estate immediately.

A family pot trust is recognized in all states and enables you to disburse funds as needed for your children. Because you cannot know in advance what those needs may be, this is a good way to take care of them. In your will, you would specify that a pot trust is to be created, then designate a trustee and name the children as the beneficiaries.

The named trustee is given the right to dispense the assets as needed and according to his or her discernment. Generally, all of the family assets are put into the pot trust so that the beneficiaries can receive benefits needed to accomplish specific goals, such as education.

A pot trust is generally dispensed with when the youngest child reaches the age of 18 (21 or 25 are also common in some states), which is why you may want to create more than one trust for older children. This way, the older ones can also receive benefits as they need them, or a certain amount of money may be designated by the grantor to be given by the trustee to each of the children for college education.

One great feature of this type of trust is that it can provide for unforeseen needs. If, for instance, the youngest child has special medical needs, then it would be necessary to take a larger portion of the estate for his or her needs. It makes more money available for the needy child, as it would be if the parents were still alive. Once the youngest child reaches the designated age, the remaining assets are divided and distributed to each of them.

In a family pot trust, the trustee needs to regularly file taxes and report how the assets were used for the year. All of the assets can be used for support, medical, and education costs.

Special Trust Issues for Medicaid

Being able to receive the benefits of Medicare and Medicaid can bring on some problems in your retirement years. For one thing, Medicare does not provide for long-term care in a nursing home. Medicaid does, but it is only for low-income people. In order to make sure that your assets are not totally consumed to meet the terms of Medicaid, you need to know that there are still some legal ways to be able to pass some of your assets to your heirs. This must be done in advance; sometimes, if you plan on setting up a trust, it must be done at least five years prior to receiving any Medicaid benefits.

Special trusts can be used when you are considering making preparations to claim Medicaid benefits. Since many forms of accounts, trusts, securities, and retirement plans are counted in terms of assets that a person holds, the government has expanded the forms that may be held and still not be counted as assets. Here are some of them.

A Testamentary Trust

This trust, which is formed when your spouse passes away, is created from the actions prescribed in a will. Since these assets were not placed into a trust by the surviving spouse's directions, they are not counted in with the assets of the spouse concerning Medicaid.

Another problem that may arise is the amount of income that the trust generates for the spouse. This should be discussed with an estate planner to find out the latest limits. Having too much income may once again interfere with the spouse's ability to receive Medicaid benefits.

Trusts for the Disabled Under 65

Disabled people who are under the age of 65 can create their own trust and not have it held against them when it comes to receiving Medicaid benefits. A number or restrictions apply, but a disabled person can create a trust that has limited distribution to himself or herself, and it must be irrevocable. After he or she reaches 65, however, this type of trust cannot be started.

The disabled can hold other trusts, too. The intent of the trust is merely designed to supplement Medicaid and other benefits. There is some rather strict wording on these types of trusts, but they generally must declare that the state in which Medicaid benefits are received will be paid back from the trust once the beneficiary dies. This is true even where more than one state is involved.

One key factor with other trusts is that the Medicaid recipient cannot create them. They need to have what is called a "third-party" origination. Because some of these situations can vary from one state to another, and from one year to the next, it is essential that you talk to an estate planner who is current with any legislation that may be relevant.

For trusts for the disabled created prior to the 65th birthday, funds added to the account do not receive the same benefits as those prior to that age. This type of trust cannot be created once an individual turns 65 years old.

Miller Trusts

Miller Trusts, also called Qualified Income Trusts (QuITs), are named after a legal case that took place in Colorado in 1990, *Miller v. Ibarra*. The case dealt with the difference between what Medicaid provides and the amount of income that a Medicaid recipient can have. This trust can be named as the recipient of a pension plan, Social Security, or other forms of income. It is used to supplement Medicaid while benefits are received; after the death of the beneficiary, the remaining assets are used to pay back the Medicaid benefits.

A Miller trust is used in states where there is a maximum amount that is placed on the income level that a Medicaid recipient can have. Income is placed into a Miller trust to qualify one for Medicaid, and to pay Medicaid back when the person dies. It also enables the spouse still at home to retain more and have a higher subsistence level.

A Medicaid recipient does not need to place all of his or her income into the Miller trust in order to qualify for those benefits. Income that is placed into the trust, however, is not actually counted as income. The balance that comes directly to the individual, however, cannot exceed the maximum allowed in that state.

Any money that is left over after Medicaid costs are recovered will go to the beneficiaries named in the trust, if there are any. Two other qualifications necessary for a Miller trust are:

1. It must be irrevocable

2. It must apply to more than one state, in case you move

Before a state will qualify an individual who moves from another state, there must be provisions in the Miller trust that would enable payment to be made to each state that provides Medicaid benefits.

Disabled Child Trusts

One loophole that you can use and still qualify for Medicaid would be to put some of your assets into a trust created for your disabled child.

Since that child will need to continue to have support after you get on Medicaid, this is permissible. Funds removed from your own assets and placed into a disabled child's account are not counted in your resources, and therefore, will not affect your ability to get Medicaid.

Extreme care needs to be taken when you do this, however, because of complications that it may cause for the child later on. If worded incorrectly, or if funds can be withdrawn from this trust for the support of your child, then it could totally negate his or her ability to get Medicaid later. There are certain phrases that cannot be used, and other ones that must be put in, in order to help your child later on. Assets remaining after the child's death will be used to repay the government and state for Medicaid expenses.

CASE STUDY: LINNEA J. LEVINE

Law Offices of Linnea J. Levine, P.C.
32 Elm Place Rye, New York, NY 10580
Tel: 914-481-5555
1071 Post Rd East, Westport, CT 06880
Tel: 203-557-0850

In most of our wills we include a discretionary special needs trust that will hold testamentary assets in the event the named beneficiary is fully disabled (not able to be gainfully employed at any type of employment due to his or her disability).

Without this language, the bequest must be given to the disabled person who then loses Medicaid eligibility. This means that the money goes to medical creditors. In order to preserve Medicaid eligibility, If the disabled beneficiary is under age 65 he can transfer the funds into a "payback" special needs trust which will provide for goods and services not paid for by Medicaid and other federal government benefits. However, upon the death of the disabled beneficiary, the remaining trust funds are paid the government as recovery of Medicaid benefits paid to the disabled beneficiary over his lifetime. It is generally more expensive to set up the payback trust, because it has to be set up by a parent of the disabled, a

CASE STUDY: LINNEA J. LEVINE

guardian, or a court. Often a court hearing is required where the state has the opportunity to appear and challenge parts of the trust.

If the funds go into the discretionary special needs trust in his parent's will, the disabled beneficiary qualifies for Medicaid and the trustee has full discretion to pay for goods and services that improve the quality of life of the disabled beneficiary. Upon the death of the disabled beneficiary, remaining trust funds are distributed to remainder beneficiaries named in the trust and not to the government.

Many individuals and families are not aware of special needs trusts. Further, there is the "conventional wisdom" that it is better and cheaper to avoid probate. Therefore, a parent will often place all of his or her assets in joint name with a healthy child with the understanding that the healthy child will provide for the disabled child. The legal reality is that upon the parent's death, the assets pass completely to the healthy child. The healthy child may have a moral obligation, but not a legal obligation, to give anything to the disabled child.

The disabled child then must bring a costly equitable action for constructive trust and a legal action for conversion. The case will hinge on available factual evidence of the deceased parent's intent and agreement with the healthy child. Some states have a "Dead Man's Statute" which prevents testimony about what the deceased told the plaintiff about his testamentary plan. This type of litigation takes a minimum of two years for discovery and to move through the court system. The cost can be several hundred thousand dollars since the healthy child has the funds to hire a large law firm with an experienced legal team to defend the case.

Even if there are no disabled beneficiaries at the time the will is drafted, if a parent lives to be age 90, his 75-year-old child could be disabled on the date of the parent's death.

The law practice of Linnea Levine concentrates on estate planning, elder law, special needs planning, guardian and conservator proceedings and accounts, and probate and estate administration.

We have litigated issues in these areas of law in both the state and federal courts in New York and Connecticut. However, we see litigation as a last resort for the reasons stated above. As Ben Franklin said, "An ounce of prevention is worth a pound of cure." Feel free to contact my office at **www.linnealevine.com** if you require additional information.

Tax Benefits From a Trust

Whether you can save money by forming a trust will probably depend on how much money or assets you have. This is partly because there are a number of fees involved, and it also depends on what kind of trust you are talking about.

It is possible that if you are not dealing with much money, the costs required to administer the trust could outweigh the tax savings gained from the process. These costs include:

- Preparation of annual tax returns

- Cost of maintaining the account

- Cost of making distributions

All costs will need to be considered so you are not spending more than what you gain by having the trust. An estate planner can help you understand the taxes involved in going through probate versus the cost of getting and maintaining a trust.

Other forms of trusts are no good when it comes to bringing you savings from taxes. In those cases, the benefit is generally to enable a grantor the power to exert some control over the assets of the estate in some way after passing away. This could be for the preservation of the assets over a long term, it could be for the benefit of others not old enough to use them yet, or it could be for a specific purpose, such as education or medical reasons. Of course, almost any other purpose is good, too, since a trust can be modified to suit any legal purpose.

Trusts can be a very effective tool in reducing your estate taxes, if you have the right kind and if they are working in conjunction with your will. In order to ensure that it is done correctly, you need to work with an estate planning lawyer to discuss all your needs.

Trusts are generally not taxable simply because the assets in them are not part of the probate process. However, certain terms and conditions may apply. One example is that of a life insurance trust. The proceeds from a life insurance policy can only be estate-tax exempt when there are no controls on the trust by the grantor, or any benefits that he or she receives from it for three years prior to the death of the grantor. If there are any benefits to the grantor during that time period, it all will go to the estate and become disqualified for tax exemption. This means that much of it will be removed for estate taxes.

If the grantor retains any control over the trust at all, then it is treated as the property of the grantor. It is even possible for an irrevocable trust to be classified as a grantor trust, too. This means that the grantor will have to claim any interest gained from the trust as income.

14
The Qualified Interminable Interest Property (QTIP)

When you are looking for a special trust that gives you limited use with tax avoidance, you may want to consider the Qualified Interminable Interest Property (QTIP). Its greatest benefit, however, may be to those who are on their second marriage with children involved from previous marriages.

QTIPs were created a number of years ago because, up until that time, there was no way for a tax exemption to occur without the removal of asset control. Any assets that were to enjoy being exempt from taxes had to be passed on to the surviving spouse and placed under that person's control without restriction. It had to become completely his or her own. Of course, when that happened, that spouse could then determine the future of those assets. The deceased spouse could have no further say in the matter.

This did not go over very well, and spouses needed a way to both provide for the surviving spouse and still have control over the assets after death. All too often, the assets were finding their way into the pockets of the children from the first marriage of the surviving spouse. There was nothing (or little) being given to his or her own children.

At that time, no tax exemption was permitted unless the surviving spouse had received total control of the assets. In most cases, this allowed it to be placed under her control and then she would do with those assets as desired, often without regard for the deceased husband's wishes. Sometimes it also occurred that the surviving husband was doing the same thing. Eventually, the QTIP was created as the solution to this dilemma. It took care of the following needs:

- Met qualifications for tax exemption on transfer to spouse

- Provided income for surviving spouse until death

- Was given to the appointed beneficiaries of the first spouse to die

The following is a closer look at each of these details.

Qualified for Tax Exemption

Because the QTIP trust was designed to meet the problems that were not resolved with other instruments of asset transfer, this instrument successfully met those needs and still enabled the desired tax break. This means that there are no taxes when the assets are transferred to the surviving spouse in a QTIP.

There will be taxes, however, when the surviving spouse passes away. The children will get a tax bill, and so will others who succeed them.

Provides Income for Surviving Spouse

When the surviving spouse needs an income, this is an excellent way to provide for it.

There are two ways that this takes care of the survivor. First, all of the interest goes to the surviving spouse. This is one of the main tenets of the QTIP, and it does not matter where the interest comes from. If there is property that is bringing in rent money, and interest is gained, it must go to the spouse.

Second, the QTIP provides that the interest cannot be given to anyone else. This assures that it goes to the right person for the right purpose, for life. It cannot be diverted to anyone else for any reason.

These provisions ensure that the assets, and the interest from them, are given solely for the benefit and maintenance of the spouse. Of course, the benefit is of value only while the spouse is alive; after that, the assets go where they were originally intended.

Given to Appointed Beneficiaries of First Spouse

After the surviving spouse dies, the assets are passed on to the original beneficiaries named by the first spouse. This means that even though the first spouse had passed away, he or she still retained control over the assets even though they were passed on to the surviving spouse. Although the spouse received benefits of the assets, it was only in a limited way.

The real benefit of a QTIP trust is that the original designation of the deceased spouse is carried out, and taxes are still avoided. Therefore, if you have other purposes in mind, a QTIP may not be for you.

One other benefit is that it will keep the assets from even the possibility that a new spouse could gain control. If the surviving spouse should remarry, then the assets would still remain under the control of the surviving spouse only, and go to the appointed beneficiaries after his or her death.

Special Uses of the QTIP

The QTIP trust could also come in handy in the case of a surviving stepparent who is not liked by the children of the new marriage partner. The children of the deceased partner could try to interfere and grab all of their parent's assets, leaving the surviving partner with nothing.

A QTIP is designed to prevent leaving the surviving spouse with nothing, and keeps the goods out of the hands of greedy children who want their inheritance now. It places the assets away from their hands and ensures that the surviving spouse has the needed maintenance as long as he or she is alive.

Further assurance is provided when the trustee is a third-party entity, not a relative. Trustee designation could be anyone, but greater safety is obtained when you use a bank or trust company for the dispersion of the interest to the spouse and then all the assets upon death.

This estate planning tool is not that useful for those who are in their first marriage and have no children other than from the marriage. In fact, there is no reason to use a QTIP under those circumstances, and a will could accomplish most of their needs.

Potential Problems That a QTIP May Cause

There is hardly any instrument that is without at least one problem, and not every instrument will work for everyone. QTIPs fall into this category as well, and their potential problems need to be considered before you settle on the notion that it will solve all your needs.

Appraisal Rate

One of the main concerns is that a QTIP provides the tax-free transfer of assets to the surviving spouse. The assets' value, however, are where a problem arises. The assets are entered into the QTIP trust at current value — and at that value, there are no taxes.

When these same assets are passed to the children, however, they do so with the new appraised value, meaning even more taxes will be due. It also means that a smaller estate is passed on to the heirs. It is, however, a much larger share than would have been passed on if the inheritance tax had been paid twice.

When a QTIP's assets are transferred to the beneficiaries after the death of the surviving spouse, estate taxes will be taken out of the trust. These taxes, however, will be at the highest percentage allowable.

Medical Benefits

A potential problem may occur with a QTIP in the event of prolonged illness. This may require additional thought concerning the use of this instrument.

If the surviving spouse has his or her own assets, separate from the deceased, it is possible that a prolonged illness may consume them. Then, in order for this spouse to apply for governmental health benefits, he or she would need to declare the funds in the QTIP. This declaration could make it impossible to obtain health benefits, depending on what laws govern this determination at that time.

Possible Solutions

In some cases, or to prevent possible scenarios, it may be necessary to put certain clauses in the QTIP documents. These clauses could include statements that would declare some circumstances under which the principal, or a portion of it, may and may not be used. This type of clause, often called a "spendthrift clause," could also be used to keep the assets out of the hands of creditors.

15
Limited Partnerships

Wen you have a business that you want to pass on to successive family members, a limited partnership may be the estate planning tool you need. Depending on your intent for the business and its assets, there are several forms of limited partnerships that you can choose from. This would include the family limited partnership and the charitable limited partnership; we will discuss each in detail after this overview of limited partnerships.

The Advantages of a Limited Partnership

A limited partnership is a great tool for passing on the wealth of the originators of the business — generally to their children. Any assets that are placed in the partnership will enjoy some benefits, as will the creators and the heirs. Here are some of the benefits of a limited partnership.

Retain Control

The creators of the limited partnership usually become the general partners. This enables them (one or more) to retain control of the assets and use them as long as they are alive. They can also buy or sell property and add or remove assets while they are alive.

This control over the assets also pertains to anything that is bought or sold. The general partners are able to choose how to distribute assets that are gained from the sale of property, as well. As you can see, the level of control that the general partners retain is the same as though it still belonged to them. The limited partners, who are usually the children or heirs, do not have a part in the decision-making processes of a limited partnership.

Limited Taxes

Taxes are greatly reduced for the general partners, and very limited on the part of limited partners. Because some of the assets are distributed among the limited partners, the taxes are also distributed, and each partner pays the taxable amounts on the assets and distributions that are under his or her control. A limited partnership is not taxable as an entity.

A limited partnership is considered to be a "flow-through" agency, which means that it merely directs assets through it to the use or control of others. The amount of control that is given to each partner will determine the amount of taxes that each partner is responsible for. He or she is responsible for paying taxes on any distributions that are received as a partner.

Maximum Advantage

In order to get the greatest advantage from a limited partnership situation, assets need to be placed into it immediately. You should know, however, that it is never to your advantage to put all of your assets into one instrument for safekeeping. Laws can change and make one instrument become ineffective over time. The greatest safety lies in placing your assets into a number of instruments, and possibly even in different states.

The IRS has negated some limited partnerships because some people failed to put assets into them. After some of your assets are placed into the limited partnership, then you need to distribute them. You have the greatest safety when you have about 99 percent of those assets distributed to the limited partners.

Remember that the general partner has unlimited liability. All assets will remain under your control and will stay there until you die, or if you remove them from the limited partnership. It is also very important to remember, however, that any assets that remain under the control of the general partner can be subject to litigation. This is why the widest distribution possible to the limited partners will provide you with the greatest amount of safety.

Further, you will also enjoy the largest tax reduction possible once you distribute these assets. The burden for future taxes gets placed on the recipient of the assets: the limited partners. While you enjoy no taxes, they will most likely enjoy a lower tax rate because they would have a lower income level.

A further tax reduction, however, will come to the general partners simply because they do not actually control the assets that they possess. This enables you to discount the value of the assets transferred by up to about 40 percent of the value of the assets. The key here is control.

A WORD OF CAUTION

It would be a very good idea to have an outside appraiser come and appraise all valuable assets that you are going to place into the limited partnership. This puts your estimated value beyond question and may help you if the IRS ever calls these matters into question.

A further problem can be avoided if you do not try to exempt more than about 60 percent of the value of the assets that are distributed. This seems to be about the limit that the IRS will tolerate. Go above that level and you will probably be hearing from them, and then they will have a very close look at everything.

Creditor Protection

Each of the partners receives a degree of protection from the limited partnership. There is limited liability for the limited partners and an unlimited liability for the general partners.

Limited partners cannot be held responsible for their personal debt, except to the limit of their percentage of the assets. Even then, about all that can happen is that a creditor may be able to get a "charge order," which means that the distribution of assets that would normally come to that specific partner would go to the creditor, but only until the debt is satisfied.

A creditor cannot get control of the limited partnership, nor will the creditor get anything if there are no assets being distributed. The main reason for the safety from creditors is that a partnership cannot be charged for the debt of an individual. However, you do need to keep in mind that a general partner has unlimited liability. A general partner can place assets beyond the reach of creditors only if those assets have been distributed to the limited partners. Otherwise, all assets under the general partner not distributed may be up for grabs by creditors.

Setting Up the Limited Partnership

Limited partnerships need to be set up in a way that carefully follows the IRS regulations for them. In recent years, the IRS has been watching limited partnerships in order to find flaws; when it finds them, it discounts the limited partnership altogether. If your limited partnership were not recognized by the IRS, it would mean that an enormous amount of taxes would become suddenly due, and with interest.

Business Purposes Only

The main thing the IRS looks for is the business aspect of the limited partnership. If the IRS determines that it is not for a strictly business purpose, then it is considered to be for the purpose of tax evasion. The only way to avoid this is to follow the rules the IRS sets forth for limited partnerships.

The business purpose of your partnership may be partly determined by some of the assets that are put into it. If you put, for instance, your own personal house into it, that cannot serve any business use, at least not as the IRS would see it. Other assets that you should not put into it would include personal possessions or property that have no business purpose. Merely having the wrong possessions under the control of your limited partnership may be all that is needed to indicate that your limited partnership is not purely for business.

Business Operations Only

Another thing that determines whether your limited partnership, or family limited partnership, has a business use is the way it conducts its business affairs. You need to have regular business meetings and guidelines for both general and limited partners, and the limited partnership should be operating within the dictates of the documents that created it. It is a good idea to create minutes of your regularly scheduled meetings, too, as a way to verify that they are being held.

Other Requirements

A limited partnership also must do a couple of other things in order to retain its legal status. The first of these is that there are annual fees that must be paid each year. Just like a business that has to renew its license each year and pay taxes, a limited partnership must also pay annual fees. If you want to keep your legal status as a legitimate business, these fees will have to be regularly paid on time.

A second requirement for a limited partnership is that the general partners cannot retain any control over any distributed assets where a tax reduction has been claimed. There also must be an immediate benefit for the limited partner who receives the distribution. Future benefits do not count.

Family Limited Partnerships

In essence, a family limited partnership (FLP) is simply a limited partnership that is being used to protect the assets of a family and put them into a partnership situation. The exact same rules apply in this situation as in the above. Technically, there is no such entity as an FLP, except in the minds of the estate planners; the IRS will treat it as a limited partnership.

You can almost be sure of trouble with the IRS if you create an FLP and you are both the general partner and the limited partner. To them, this will appear to be a simple case of tax evasion.

It is very important when you create an FLP that you use a knowledgeable estate planner who knows the laws of your state. The IRS is looking for any flaws, and this could be an area where one may exist, and you may not even know it. You are far better off paying an expert to prepare it correctly for you in order to stay above suspicion.

You also want to be very careful of any estate planner who will use a generic form for the creation of your FLP. While it may be all you need, it is questionable whether that particular estate planner has your best interests in mind. Good estate planning means that each situation needs to be fitted to your unique needs. A generic form may not allow such distinctiveness.

Charitable Limited Partnerships

A charitable limited partnership is an FLP that has a charitable aspect attached to it. However, these organizations, also called CHAR-FLiPs, are under an even greater level of scrutiny by the IRS.

One reason for this scrutiny is that it is so easy to designate the "gifts" in such a way that it becomes obvious that there is very little benefit to the charitable organization. When this happens, it is just a fancy name for tax evasion to the IRS.

A CHAR-FLiP is usually set up so that some charitable organization, usually a 501(c)(3), agrees to the terms. The way this most frequently happens is that a piece of property is donated to the charity for a designated number of years, and at a greatly reduced price. Then, when the time is up, the land is repurchased at a much lower price. In order to do this, however, the charity must be willing to become a limited partner of the CHAR-FLiP.

This type of agreement is often made with the understanding that there may be a donation of a certain size once the property is repurchased in the future. Other than this, however, many CHAR-FLiPs will not participate because they either feel that there is too little advantage for them, or they do not want to become a limited partner and have the added responsibilities and taxes that go with it.

Another problem that the IRS looks at is how much the donor benefits from the transaction and how much the beneficiary benefits. If there is a large offset in value on the side of the donor, then it appears to be an obvious case of tax evasion. The result would most likely be that the donor would be given a tax bill for the difference in values.

The size of the income that the general partner receives while managing the CHAR-FLiP will also be examined. If it is large, then once again the real beneficiary is revealed.

A simple way to avoid any real problems with the IRS would be to sell the property outright and then give the proceeds directly to the charitable agency. This will, of course, limit the reduction in taxes, but it will also make the IRS happy. When things are done this way, there is no question about motive or intent in the gifts given. Any property that is given should also have a clear and immediate benefit to the charity, as well as be appraised first. This also means that the gift will need to be of value to the nature of the charity.

16
Gift Giving

One of the easiest ways to place your assets into the hands of your children and other loved ones is through gift giving. It is one of the simplest methods, too, with the least amount of complications. This makes it convenient for all involved and a method of estate planning that should not be overlooked.

Since you have an exemption from gift and estate taxes up to $2 million per person, and $4 million per couple, it is a good way to reduce your own taxes and be a blessing to someone else. In fact, by putting gifts of money into the hands of others, you could bless many people. This amount will go up to $3.5 million per individual in the year 2009. By making giving a tool that is part of your estate planning program, you can give an even larger portion to your heirs and less to the IRS.

General Rules for Gift Giving

When you give gifts to someone, or even to a charitable organization, you need to be aware that there may be taxes involved. For the most part, the rules are rather clear for simple gifts. More complex rules can apply, however, if you give in ways that do not fall into one of the following categories.

Gift-Tax Exemption Limit of $1 Million

The first rule to affect your generosity through gift giving is the total amount that you can give. The government has a limit of $1 million on gifts you can give to others that are considered part of your gift-tax exemption. This is for your whole lifetime. Neither the donor nor the recipient will pay taxes on any amount that falls under this classification. This is a fixed amount that will not change, as in the case of the estate tax exclusion amount.

You do need to be aware, though, that if the gift in any way earns interest, or brings in a profit, then there will be tax on that amount above the original gift value. While this will not be a concern to the donor, it may be a problem to the recipient, especially if that increase is not available to help pay those additional taxes. This means that the donor should consider the needs of the recipient before giving the gifts so that the tax costs can also be provided for, if necessary.

No Limits on Giving to Spouse

One of the nice things that the IRS has done is to allow people to give an infinite amount of gifts to his or her spouse. There is no estate or gift tax involved whatsoever. This allows you to reduce your estate tax free. The goal in this case would be to allow as little as possible to go into your estate, thus reducing your taxes greatly. However, if you desire to pass all of your possessions to your spouse, then it really is a moot point. Simply leave it in your will; it will still be tax free.

Annual Gift Limits

Apart from the above situations, an individual can still give to anyone he or she wants, as long as one simple criterion exists. Your gifts will need to be limited to $12,000 per individual per year. A husband and a wife could each give that amount, which would bring that amount up to $24,000. There are no limits, though, on the amount of people that you can give this amount (or less) to. Therefore, you could give gifts of $12,000 to 50 people (or more) in a single year, and then repeat it the next year and the next. Neither party would owe any gift taxes on that amount.

The $12,000 is on a per-person basis. Thus, if both the husband and the wife wanted to give the same person $12,000 each, then a total of $24,000 can be given tax free. After the limit of $12,000 has been reached, any amount above that is counted and subtracted from both the gift-tax exemption amounts and the estate tax exclusion limits.

This gift amount, as long as it stays under the $12,000 per-person per-year category, does not affect your $1 million gift-tax exemption. This means you can give it away free each year. Obviously, you would want to keep careful records on all gifts given. You need to include the person and the amounts, as well as general information, like dates and totals, in case the IRS should ask.

There Must Be a Present Interest

In order to qualify as a gift to an individual, it needs to have a present interest. This means that the recipient must have immediate access to the monetary gift. If you are counting the amount as part of your gift-tax exemption limit, then this also applies. Even if the recipient is a minor, he or she needs to have full control of the gift immediately.

Exceptions to Gift-Giving Limits

Giving your money to individuals cannot be much simpler, but there are some ways in which you could give even more — if you desire. One way would be to pay directly any amount toward an individual's medical or education bills. The necessary element here is that it cannot go through that person's hands, but must be paid directly to that institution in his or her name. Money that is given toward education must be applied to the tuition and cannot include extras, like books.

If you should still want to give a gift to the individual apart from that, you can, because money given to hospitals or colleges does not affect the $12,000 figure at all. You can still give a gift of this amount, even though you may have paid any amount to an institution for him or her.

Other Types of Education Gifts for Consideration

Several avenues are open when you want to consider giving a gift to pay for a child or grandchild's education. You do not even need to wait until he or she is in college before you can give. After all, gifts may need to be given quickly to reduce your estate for tax purposes.

A great option would be to prepay for the child's education by putting the money into a college savings plan. Often referred to as 529 plans, they come in various forms. For instance, you can give your money to your state's 529 plan on behalf of your grandchild. This means you could either pay into a state-sponsored program ("savings" type of account), or you can go with a particular college 529 "prepaid" program. Generally, the prepaid programs are for that college only, but a state 529 plan can be used just about anywhere, possibly even overseas. You could even buy into another state's 529 plan, if you think your student will attend a college there.

One advantage of the "prepaid" plan is that it enables you to eliminate rising college costs. It does this by giving you tomorrow's education at today's prices. You buy either by the classes or by the year, and the tuition is then paid for at that time. After the money is in the account, it starts earning interest, and the interest should cover any increase in costs. This provides you with a good hedge against inflation and still makes your gift able to cover an equivalent amount of education.

If you are not sure where your family member might go to college, or even if he or she will go, then the more general type of program (state's plan) would work best in your situation. On the other hand, some colleges provide matching funds if your descendant attends that particular school. One advantage is that you can easily change the name of a beneficiary if you want or need to.

The money that you put into a 529 plan is immediately deducted from your estate. This provides you with the tax break you want, and also provides for some assurance that your money will go toward your child or grandchild's education. If you decide that you need the money for medical reasons (or anything), you can take the money out. At that time, it enters into the taxable part of your estate.

You may want to keep in mind what will happen in the event of your death. When you apply for the account, you should appoint a successor. This individual will become the total owner, even to the point of being able to withdraw all of the money in the account. Unless you trust that individual to use your money where you intended, you need to make provisions for it. One possible option is to ensure that your 529s are placed under a trust when you die.

It is better to keep the 529 account in your own name, rather than in the student's name, because if kept in your name, it should not interfere with the student's ability to get further financial aid. The student would need to report it if it were in his or her name.

Limitations on Other Education Gifts

You will probably find that a 529 plan will give you more flexibility than other plans. This includes plans such as the Uniform Transfers to Minors Act (UTMA), the Uniform Gifts to Minors Act (UGMA), or the Coverdell Plan. The Coverdell Plan, for instance, will only allow you to put $2,000 into it each year; but the money can also be used to pay for elementary and high school education. If you intend to place less than $2,000 into the account, then this could be a good option for you. The other two plans must be reported by the student, meaning that they most likely will affect his or her ability to get financial aid.

A 529 plan, on the other hand, allows you to place much larger amounts into it, and in some states, there is no limit. You may also place into it — at one time — a single gift of $60,000. This is equal to your gifts for one person for five years. The only catch is that you cannot add any more to it, tax free, until the five years is past. After that, you can still add your annual gift amount of $12,000 per person.

Another thing that you could do is to place money into more than one type of education savings program. For instance, if you already had a 529 plan and a Coverdell, money could be put into these accounts for the same person. This would allow you to split the money, possibly putting $2,000 in the Coverdell and $10,000 into the 529 plan. You need to know, however, that the total must not exceed the $12,000 personal gift, or you would be required to pay gift taxes on any amount above that, unless your spouse also makes a donation.

A Word of Caution About Personal Gifts

You could experience some problems if the gift is not subtracted from your estate immediately. For instance, a problem may occur if the check is written but not yet cashed at the time of death. In that case, it remains part of the estate and is subject to estate taxes. A simple way around this problem is to write cashier's checks, which subtract the cash immediately.

How to Use Personal Gifts to Rapidly Decrease Your Estate

Placing gifts of money or property can be a very effective way to reduce your estate quickly, and still make sure it goes where you want. This should be thought about carefully, as the gift amount is out of your control completely once the gift is given. There can be no further limitations or assurances that it will last for any length of time, or that it will stay in that person's hands.

Remember, too, that the goal is only to reduce the estate to below the amount of the estate exemption amount. For two people, that amount is $4 million, but it will be raised to $7 million in 2009. After 2010, what this new amount will be cannot be predicted, because Congress will need to enact some new legislation at that time. Without new laws, this limit will drop back down to $2 million per couple and $1 million per individual — where it was in 2001.

Using the $12,000 annual gifts alone could reduce your estate very quickly, and help you avoid a large amount of taxes. For instance, if you had seven people you wanted to give money to, then you could give $12,000 to each of them, which would total $84,000 in one year. If both the husband and the wife each gave $12,000 to all seven of these relatives, then the gifts in one year now becomes a total of $168,000. If this were repeated for the next five years, then the gifts of one person would reduce the estate by $420,000, and two people would give away a total of $840,000. Of course, if desired, this could be kept up for many years, or new grandchildren or great-grandchildren could be born that would allow an even greater figure to be given annually. Remember, too, that there are no taxes paid on these gifts by either the donor or recipient.

Why You Should Start Early in Your Gift Giving

Besides having the joy of giving gifts to others and making them happy, you will receive a great deal of joy as well. This makes it a fun part of life and can actually help to secure the friendship and trust you want from those who are going to receive your assets. Apart from this, there is another reason to start your gift giving early.

The main reason is the amount that you can give away. Of course, if you do not have considerably above the personal estate tax exemption amount, then this is not a problem for you. If you do have an estate valued at considerably more than the exemption amount, you should start making gifts as soon as possible. The reason is the amount you can give away over a period of years, as opposed to what you could give away in a year or two. The example in the last section shows how much you could give away in a five-year span as opposed to a single year. The couple was able to give more than three-quarters of a million dollars, but it still took five years.

For each year that you do not give away gifts, you face a likelihood that death may come and that it will have to be placed into your estate. Once it is there, the government will gladly take a healthy portion. You also have to know that you can only give so much away in a year. With this in mind, it only makes sense that you start early, and then more can be placed tax free into the hands of those you want to have it. Otherwise, you may be forced to make gifts to agencies and other avenues that may not allow it to go to those you had hoped, just so that it does not go to the IRS.

A final thing to keep in mind about gift giving is that the estate tax exemption amounts will soon be changing. Although it will greatly increase during the years 2009 and 2010, the following year it drops back down to only $1 million for one person, unless Congress passes some new legislation. This means that you may have to begin now in order to reduce that estate to a smaller size by that time. Although it is unknown exactly what will occur at that time, it is also possible that the IRS may be collecting a good deal of money from taxes for those that did make any preparations to avoid it.

Limitations on Gift Giving

The IRS will be watching how much you give away each year. This means that they are looking to ensure that everything looks appropriate. This gives you an additional reason not to wait until the last minute to make your gifts. Here are some things that will cause you problems if found on your tax returns:

- Giving more than 50 percent of your adjusted gross income (AGI) to charitable organizations

- Giving more than 30 percent of long-term capital gain properties to public charities

- Giving more than 30 percent of your AGI to private foundations

Once again, the IRS is taking steps to ensure that people are not trying to evade taxes. This means that you should develop a life style of gift giving, rather than wait until the last minute.

One thing to beware of when giving a gift is the writing of the check. Even if you have a joint account, the husband should not write a check as a gift for more than the annual gift exclusion amount for himself. The problem is that the person writing the check is the one giving the gift, according to the IRS. Even if both the husband and wife want to give a gift of the limit — $24,000 total from both of them — and the husband writes it, then a gift tax will be due on $12,000 of it. In addition, this same amount will be deducted from the maximum gift exclusion amount of the husband. The only way around it is for separate checks to be written and signed by each married spouse.

Making Gifts with Your Will: Bequests

Another way to give last-minute gifts is to simply make a bequest with your will. Any gift given in this way will escape estate taxes. A will gives you many ways to designate the assets you want to give to a charitable organization. You can leave any type of asset, too, as long as you are the only owner. Here are a few ways you might arrange to leave some assets to this type of agency.

- **Specified amount** — You can designate exactly how much (e.g., $15,000) of any type of asset should be given to the charitable organization.

- **Percentage amount** — This gives you a degree of flexibility if you are not certain how much may be left. You may designate, for example, 25 percent of your remaining assets after the other assets have been distributed.

- **Contingent amount** — If you are uncertain about whether certain needs will be in place, such as whether your spouse will survive you, you can use this method. Wording may include,

"If I am survived by... then 75 percent of my estate will go to [him or her]." Otherwise, you might say, 50 percent goes to your children and 50 percent goes to a named charitable agency, whatever your intentions may be.

- **Residual amount** — This is especially beneficial if you know you will have medical costs and other things that may leave you with an uncertain estate size. You may state that, after your expenses and taxes are paid, then whatever is left will go to the agency of your choice.

Each of these situations enables you to make the decisions when you write the will. And remember, a will is also adjustable — simply by rewriting it or making an amendment.

A problem with this type of approach, however, is that you could enjoy greater tax benefits if you resort to some other tax-sheltering instruments. This approach does give you control of that asset, but enjoys tax breaks only after the will is executed. If you have assets larger than what the estate tax exemption will cover you for, you should consider using other methods.

In some cases, it may be better to designate percentage values as opposed to numeric amounts. In other words, it would be better to say 25 percent rather than $25,000. One reason is that, if the assets are slowly depleted, or more is depleted than initially anticipated, a percentage-based value enables all to still get a portion. Each beneficiary also receives a portion based on whether the asset value increases or decreases. Otherwise, inflexible numeric values may mean that some beneficiaries will receive their amounts, and others may not get anything.

An increase in assets will also have the same effect; each beneficiary can then enjoy a larger portion because it is not limited by specific dollar values. This could also help cover some of the loss that occurs when a specified amount goes through inflation over a longer, unknown period of time.

Special assets could also be given in this way. You might designate a portion of your IRA to either an individual or a charitable organization. You can also do the same with stock, bonds, property, a pension plan, and even part of an insurance policy.

The Uniform Gifts to Minors Act (UGMA) and the Uniform Transfers to Minors Act (UTMA)

The Uniform Gifts to Minors Act (UGMA) and the Uniform Transfers to Minors Act (UTMA) were set up to enable a donor to put money and assets into an account, like a trust, for a minor. The UGMA was established first, but was later expanded to become the UTMA. Each state, however, had the right to make the change if it wanted to do so. Not all states use the UTMA, but whether it uses the UTMA or the UGMA, they are very similar.

When this type of account is created for a minor, a trustee will need to be designated who will have control of the account until the minor comes of age. You can even place real estate into a UTMA. Assets placed into the account are deductible as gifts and are one of the ways you can place money into a minor's hands, though in a limited way.

The nice thing about this type of account is that it does not require all the formalities of drawing up paperwork for a trust. In fact, it uses the language and laws of the state you are in, and you do not need an attorney to set it up for you. Instead, you can go to a bank, a mutual fund manager, or even a stockbroker and open your UGMA or UTMA account there.

This type of account has one drawback that you will want to think about before you open it. All money that is placed into this type of account will become fully available to the beneficiary once he or she turns 18 or 21, depending on the laws in your state.

Although you may express your desires to this young person while you are living, once that age is reached, there is no legal way to enforce it. There are no guarantees that the money will be used wisely, and not even the trustee can enforce the wise use of the money once that age is reached. Nor is it possible to hide the money from the recipient, because he or she will need to sign the tax forms for it each year. For this reason, it may not be a wise move to place a large amount of money into this type of account. It will suddenly become available to a young person who may not have learned any fiscal responsibility yet, and this means it could be consumed quickly and unwisely. You may want to place large amounts of money into a trust for the young person instead (or in addition).

Another drawback, at least for some people, would be that all control of the funds must be relinquished to the trustee, who cannot turn around and give any benefits to the donor. The funds also need to be available to the child once the required age is reached. It is this feature, that the beneficiary has an immediate present interest, that makes the UGMA or UTMA able to qualify for the tax break you want. Otherwise, it would not qualify. The trustee can begin immediately using the assets for the benefit of the recipient. You should also be aware that the IRS watches these accounts carefully to make sure that there is no foul play. The donor and the trustee must not be the same person. This would pose an obvious question of the donor retaining control over the assets in the account.

So, if control is not an issue, or if you want to put some money into the account for the young person, you can use this method as a tax break.

Other money that you want to ensure gets used for your vision and the development of this young person can be placed into other financial instruments for that purpose.

This type of account may need further planning on your part in other ways. Here are several potential problems:

- A UGMA may reduce a student's availability for financial aid in college

- Money is not transferable to other accounts

- Money cannot be withdrawn by the donor, even if a need arises later

- The account belongs only to one child

The account needs to be created for only one person. What could happen is that you put a large amount of money into one child's account, thinking that much more will follow for the other children, but the additional abundance may not be there. This could create an uneven distribution that cannot be changed later.

There is some debate over whether money can be taken out of this account by the custodian for any kind of support for the child. The actual wording is such that it does allow this in some cases, but the custodian must be sure to keep accurate records of all transactions in case there is ever a question about it. The wording makes it clear that the assets are "for the use and benefit of the minor."

Taxes on a UGMA or UTMA could also be a problem, depending on the age of the child. Portions of the money are charged at different tax rates, and the so-called "kiddie tax" does apply between the ages of 14 and 18. This tax was created to prevent parents from trying to place their assets into one of their children's accounts in order to avoid paying taxes on it. The "kiddie tax" only applies to unearned income. The way it works is that the first $850 (in 2007) is tax free. After that, the next $850 is charged at the child's tax rate (about 15 percent), and whatever is above that receives the parent's tax rate.

Turning Personal Loans Into Gifts

You can make personal loans to relatives when they have a need for it. You can, of course, ultimately write off the loan as a gift if the borrower is unable to repay it. One thing that needs to be remembered, however, is that if there is no interest being charged, it is considered to be a gift, which then falls under gift tax.

One way around having to pay gift tax on a loan would be to charge the minimum interest, at the applicable federal rate (AFR), when you make the loan. The IRS sets this interest rate (the AFR) every year, and you can find the current rate on their Web site. This interest rate is the borderline between what is acceptable for a true loan and what makes it a gift. Anything less than the AFR is considered a gift by the IRS, and anything with interest equal to it or higher will qualify as a loan.

If you do not charge at least the AFR amount, then the IRS may calculate what is called an imputed interest rate. This means that the amount of the balance of the loan would be treated as if you had charged interest, and you will be taxed on this imputed tax amount.

Imputed tax is calculated as being the difference between the AFR and the amount that you actually charged. If you did not charge any interest on the loan, then you will be charged the full AFR amount and must report it on your income tax.

Another situation arises, however, if you loaned between $10,000 and

$100,000. When the loan amount is in this range, then it is possible that you do not owe anything in the way of imputed taxes. If the income from investments of the borrower was less than $1,000, you pay no taxes. The one stipulation, though, is that you need a signed statement from the borrower on how much he or she earned in interest.

Without this stipulation, parents would often "loan" money to their children and then have the children put it into investments that would earn a large amount of interest. Because it would be on a child's account, the taxes would naturally be much lower, and people would escape the higher taxes. The IRS put these loan guidelines in place to try to prevent this practice.

Loans can always be forgiven, and they often are. Remember, though, if you need to forgive a loan, that there is a limit on how much of a gift you can give to someone: $12,000 per person. Any more than this and you will need to pay gift tax on it.

17
Health Needs

G ood estate planning should also provide for one of your most valuable assets: your health. Make sure that your estate plan takes your future health needs into account. Since there is no way of telling how much you will need or for how long you may need it, your strategy and provisions need to be adequate.

Talking over the various health need possibilities with your estate planner is a must before you begin to remove assets from your estate. You will not want to make any decisions about irrevocable trusts before you have this talk.

Medicare

The Medicare program does not provide medical coverage for nursing homes, except for short terms. It starts when you reach 65 and is available to anyone who has worked most of their life. It is different than Medicaid.

Medicaid

Medicaid is given to help those that are in a low-income level, and age is not a requirement to receive general care. Since Medicare does not provide nursing home care for any length of time, Medicaid is about the only way left for many people to go.

When people get ready to apply for Medicaid, they cannot simply disburse their assets and hope that Medicaid will take them in. Although it used to be more lenient than it is now, there are some things that must be avoided when you consider applying. The first is that Medicaid looks at what assets you had up to 36 months (it used to be 30 months) before you applied. Having too many assets within that time period could easily disqualify you and make you ineligible for some time afterward. Medicaid goes even further than that — up to a total of 60 months (5 years) prior to your application — to find out whether or not you have moved assets into a trust.

If you are hoping to use Medicaid to help you through those years when you will need it for nursing home care, you should talk to an estate planner. He or she can help you make the best plans that will work for your situation. Medicaid does allow you to transfer some assets to others (such as your spouse) for their maintenance, or to a dependent or disabled child's trust, among other things. It needs to be done a certain way, however, and you must do it some time prior to applying. An example of an improper way would be to sell or give away property at less than its value or at no cost. This will get you penalized and make you ineligible for some time.

An estate planner can help you transfer your assets in the right way at the right time. There are also a number of other options that may be available in the way of trusts. An irrevocable trust, for instance, may give you a means to preserve some of your assets, if it is created at least 60 months prior. Such assets are not counted against your Medicaid eligibility, as long as you do not control them.

While no one can foresee the exact health needs that an individual may have, you can expect that some will most likely occur. Things could happen that would put you in need of some kind of long-term care situation. This could include disability, Alzheimer's disease, old age, and more. Two things that you will need, in the event that you are in need of long-term care and do not have the ability to make decisions for yourself, are a healthcare proxy and a living will.

Healthcare Proxy

A healthcare proxy is a document that designates someone to make healthcare decisions for you if you are unable to do so. This means that, if you should become either mentally unable or comatose, then your medical interests will be taken care of for you.

This document will be needed if you have special medical considerations or limitations that you want followed if you become either comatose or unable to make medical decisions for yourself. This is especially useful if you do not wish your life to be sustained by purely mechanical means. Otherwise, doctors and family members who are not aware of your medical decisions may try to order tests and very expensive treatments or care. This can also happen after you have been declared terminally ill. This document simply provides basic guidelines as to what should be done when circumstances arise that were not anticipated.

Living Will

A living will is needed in order for you to express your intent concerning what kind of treatment you want in the event of incapacitation or similar problems. This document will need to follow the guidelines provided in that state; but it still is not guaranteed that it will be carried out as prescribed.

Some hospitals and doctors may be inclined to follow a consensus of opinion from the family rather than a single document. This seems to be becoming more popular, but it is still a good idea for you to have your ideas and thoughts available. Otherwise, a doctor, hospital, or other family member may order treatments simply because they do not know to do otherwise. They may wonder, and want to carry out your plans, but only such a document could provide the needed guidelines.

Federal law now states that patients have both the right to receive information about any possible treatments, as well as the right to refuse those treatments. A living will is designed to place your clearly expressed intentions on paper so that there can be no mistake about what your intentions might be in those situations.

If there is no living will, then it may be up to whichever family members are available to make the decision. In an emergency situation, the hospital will probably have its procedures already outlined and will initiate them immediately, unless they are provided with other instructions.

Surprisingly, a wife or husband may not even be able to alter these procedures by themselves. Some states have laws indicating that there needs to be a consensus of opinion among family members. Where that is the case, one family member — even a spouse — may not be able to change this policy. In an earlier legal case (Nancy Cruzan, New Jersey), the Supreme Court decided that the hospital would continue its care of the patient unless "clear and convincing" evidence was presented that would prove that she had different intentions.

There are two kinds of living wills: statutory and nonstatutory. The statutory kind are in compliance with the states rules of living wills, and the nonstatutory are those wills that do not conform. In a situation where a doctor knows that he or she will act upon a document that is in compliance with state regulations, this will provide him or her with a greater confidence. With a nonstatutory living will, however, it may not be followed at all.

Another good reason to have a living will could be to help spare someone else from having to make the decision. Many times, people would rather not have to make such a decision for another. It is possible that your spouse could also be killed, or likewise incapacitated, in the same event that places you in need of such a decision to be made. This would leave the decision to someone else, someone that may not be aware of your intentions. A living will can provide guidelines for a decision to be made that would help him or her rest easy with the decision once it is made.

Here are two documents that you should have, if you should ever need them. Both documents are referred to as your healthcare advance directives.

Healthcare Advance Directives

Your medical care decisions need to be placed into what is called a medical healthcare directive. This includes two distinct documents, and one is not a substitute for the other. The first of these is called a living will, and the other is a healthcare power of attorney. Some states now have them available in one document, but be sure that you have both. One part without the other will not do you or your loved one much good.

The living will is the more general of these two documents. It should generally state your intentions for your medical care concerning emergency procedures and what happens if you become incapacitated.

Contents

A healthcare power of attorney is a more detailed document. In it, you want to name the person whom you want to make medical decisions for you when you can no longer make them for yourself. You also want to make your intentions clear about various issues. You may want to cover the following areas of healthcare:

- Should life be sustained through sustenance and hydration?

- What treatments do you not want?

- Do you wish to donate your organs?

- Would you like to appoint an alternate medical proxy?

It should also be pointed out that a power of attorney is not the same thing as a healthcare power of attorney. A person with general power of attorney is not allowed to make medical decisions for you. A person with healthcare power of attorney only has the power to make medical decisions.

Distribute Copies

Once these documents are prepared, you will want to distribute them to the people who need to know about it. You may want to place a copy with the following:

- Your doctor

- People with future healthcare power of attorney

- Alternate proxies

- Your will

- Your spouse and other key family members

Making Changes

Once your advance directives are established, you can make changes to them whenever you choose. Be sure that when you do, those who need a revised copy — or a new copy — have one so that they are aware of the changes.

You also want to make sure that the documents are in agreement with each other. Conflicts in these documents will probably make them both void, so you need to look them over carefully. Also, if you spend time in a different state, you may need to have one made (just in case) that fits the laws of that state.

Power of Attorney

Another document that needs to be part of effective estate planning is power of attorney. When decisions need to be made, or bills or taxes need to be paid from your estate, and you are unable, some individual will need to have power of attorney to fulfill those duties. It gives someone else legal power to conduct your business and make decisions according to preset instructions from you.

Power of attorney actually gives that person power to make legally binding decisions. This person becomes your legal representative, even before the IRS.

There are two forms of power of attorney: one is temporary and the other much more permanent. The temporary form exists only while the estate owner (the principal) is in a medically incapacitated state and is unable to make his or her own decisions. After the principal regains consciousness and a clear mind, this power is removed. In some states, this form may need to be renewed on a regular basis.

The other form of power of attorney is called durable power of attorney. It continues until it is removed or the principal dies.

One obvious reason that you need to have this person designated is because it is not automatic, no matter whom the person may be. Even a spouse cannot assume this responsibility, unless he or she is appointed by the court to hold the position on behalf of the spouse. While this is not true everywhere, it is true in some states.

When you select someone to have your power of attorney, you may select more than one person, or divide up the various powers as needed. You may choose one person to sell some property for you, and then take the power of attorney away. You may also make the power of attorney effective immediately, temporarily, or permanently.

You can also revoke or take away the power of attorney from someone, but this could be more difficult. It depends on what the document states is the purpose and powers that he or she is given. For instance, if you designate someone to have durable power of attorney when you become unable to handle your affairs properly, then there is the possibility that, when you regain capacity, you may not be able to revoke that power. It may take a court order to do so; and in some cases, the court may decline.

Unless the power of attorney is said to be durable, these persons usually lose this power if the principal is determined to have become incapacitated. This is the temporal power of attorney. Some other powers of attorney may be said to "spring" into power when the estate owner becomes incapacitated. This term, "incapacitated," should be very carefully defined in order to prevent confusion. One way to clarify when this time comes and when the powers start may be to create a small committee of three or four people, one of who should be a medical doctor.

Making the selection of who has this durable power of attorney is very important. This person will have power to do business for you and represent the principal after that appointment. He or she should be a person of character and understand how the principal feels about many things, so that he or she can conduct basic business in the same terms.

You may want to make the person with your healthcare power of attorney different from the person with the durable power of attorney. This way, there can be no confusion, and you may avoid possible problems later, if it should be the same person making decisions in both areas.

Sometimes, after a power of attorney has been initiated, the various financial and legal institutions refuse to recognize this power. That makes it next to impossible for the person with this power to carry out the business that they have been appointed to. If that happens, you need to understand that these various agencies may be trying to protect themselves from what could be fraud. In that case, you can only try to work with them through the problem. If that should fail, you will need to go to court to either get the agency to cooperate or to have them appoint a court-directed guardian for the estate. One other way around this may be to have the principal inform the banks and other agencies about his or her decision to give this person power of attorney.

Each of these things — your healthcare directive, your healthcare proxy, and your power of attorney — is part of an essential estate planning device. They help you to preserve your assets if you should become incapacitated. They are needed to complete your plan and be able to pass on that vision in case something should happen to you that is unexpected.

It is also important that you talk with your estate planner about what methods and needs there are in each of these areas before you make a general plan. Generic forms may not be specific enough for your needs and may not even be for your state — or up to date.

If you do not have someone whom you know and trust to handle your medical and financial affairs, you may want to find an agency that will do it for you. This way, you will have this part of your estate, and your health needs, taken care of.

Conservatorships

If you should become comatose or unable to handle your own affairs, and there is no one who has been appointed with power of attorney, then the court must be petitioned by family members and a conservator or adult guardian will be appointed. This person has the legal right to manage the person's affairs as directed by the court.

Some safeguards are in place that will make the conservator responsible to the court. For one, the potential conservator will be interviewed by a court investigator, usually an attorney, and informed of his rights and responsibilities as a conservator. This person may need to become bonded as a further protection against misuse of the powers of a guardianship, which is paid for out of the estate.

Another protection for the estate is that the conservator must file paperwork detailing some of his or her actions, at least on a biannual basis. The permission of the court will also need to be obtained before certain actions are performed, such as the sale of property.

The need for a conservator — as well as the appointment of one, if needed — is up to the judge. It often will be the spouse or an adult child. There is room for a rejection by the family, however, of either the conservatorship or the appointment of a specific conservator, but this must be done at a hearing and the objector must be present. When making the choice of a conservator, there is generally a state-appointed list that needs to be followed in sequence. It is also possible that a professional conservator may be appointed. Sometimes, families prefer that there be an alternative to the conservatorship, because the proceedings and decisions are then open to the public.

The conservator is responsible for handling the financial needs of the conservatee and to seek the best care for him or her. Unless appointed by the judge to do so, though, the conservator for financial matters (conservator of the estate) is not the same person as the one responsible for the health decisions of the conservatee (conservator of the person). The one making the medical decisions (conservator of the person) will need to get permission from the court for all major medical decisions.

Some of the specific responsibilities of a conservator include:

- Taking inventory of all assets

- Paying bills

- Managing finances

- Protecting income and assets

- Investing money of conservatee

- Ensuring all benefits available are obtained

- Filing tax returns

Even though a conservatorship may not be the preferred choice, it may be the safest. With the court holding the conservator responsible, this could greatly eliminate many potential problems and disagreements that might otherwise occur among family members.

One setback, however, is that court meetings with conservators and the appointment of one can be rather costly. You can avoid these costs if your health directives and power of attorney are established in advance of the need.

The conservator is often unpaid for these duties, if he or she is a relative. Payment may be given, however, if the court is petitioned for it. Records need to be given of activities performed with time estimates involved. The court may then decide to provide payment out of the estate, but it will usually be partially based on experience and performance of specific duties.

The conservator has no power to enforce his own opinion or powers over the will of the conservatee. The conservatee, if not comatose, still has certain rights, too. These rights include the power to:

- Make or change the will

- Have a lawyer

- Get married

- Ask the judge to change the conservator

- Seek to end the conservatorship

- Control salary

- Control spending (unless a judge refuses this right)

- Vote

- Make healthcare decisions

The conservator also has some responsibilities. To sum them up, the conservator is responsible for the overall welfare of the conservatee and must give him or her the greatest freedom. The responsibilities of the conservator include:

- Healthcare

- Food

- Clothes and personal care

- Residence — cannot move the conservatee out of state

- Recreation

One thing that the conservator of the person cannot do is to contradict the conservatee when it comes to medical treatments. If the conservatee says "no," the decision is final.

18
Other Possibilities

Although a number of options for transferring wealth to your children or grandchildren have already been discussed, there are a few more that you should know about. Each of them could have a place in your estate planning program, enabling you to have the power and flexibility you want.

Pay-on-Death Bank Accounts

Any bank account that has a pay-on-death option is a good choice to get around estate taxes. It avoids going into probate and is transferred to the person named when the account holder dies. You retain full control of the assets while you are alive, and all assets go to the named individual with full rights after you die. The beneficiary does not have access to any of the assets in the account until your death.

You can name a beneficiary of your choice when you open the account. One potential problem, though, is that you can only name one beneficiary, so there are no alternates. You can, however change the name of the beneficiary at any time. As soon as the death is proven to the bank officials, the money is theirs.

This could be an efficient way to leave money for your funeral and other needs immediately following your death. Any money you have in a will becomes secured and unavailable until settlement, which could occur many months, and maybe even years, later.

You can create a number of these accounts for each person you want to receive the assets in them. This eliminates the need for any attorney, probate, or taxes.

This type of bank account gives you a great advantage over a joint account. Once you open a joint account with another individual, then that person has the right to withdraw any assets that are in the account. This could create a serious problem if you have need of that money. The beneficiary, however, cannot use money put into a pay-on-death account until you are deceased.

Pay-on-Death Securities

This works the exact same way as a pay-on-death bank account. You name one beneficiary to receive the securities, and when you die, they receive them. This removes the estate taxes from them for your estate, but taxes will need to be paid by the recipient.

Pay-on-Death Real Estate

This is the same situation as above. You can place a beneficiary's name on the deed, allowing the transfer to be free of any estate taxes. This bypasses your estate, enabling the property to stay clear of probate.

Other assets that allow you to name a beneficiary also have the same status. This can make life simple. More people are using this as a way to do their estate planning at no cost to themselves. A similar phrase to "pay-on-death" or "payable-on-death" that has the same effect is "transfer-on-death."

Tenancy by the Entirety

When property is owned by more than one person, it may be called a joint tenancy. In many cases, when one of the owners wants to sell his or her portion of the property, then it must be sold and each person receives his or her share. A tenancy by the entirety, however, has one other stipulation that does not exist in other common tenancy situations: the owners must be married.

Property owned in a marital state means that each of the joint owners has equal right to the entire property. For that reason, it is necessary for both to agree on a transaction before any can be made. When one spouse dies, it becomes the property of the other.

Tenancy by the entirety is an excellent protection against creditors in states that are not community property. A creditor cannot go after the property of both, when only one of the married partners is responsible for the debt. However, in a community property state, they can. You will need to see whether you are living in a community property state so that you know which laws apply to you. Currently, only about half of the states accept a tenancy by the entirety situation.

One problem that can occur is that property in a tenancy by the entirety cannot be put into a trust upon the death of one of the property owners. This means that you will be faced immediately with estate taxes on the property when the other spouse dies. One way around this would be to have the surviving spouse reject the inheritance. This will enable it to be placed into a trust.

Community Property With Right of Survivorship (CPWROS)

This form of owning property is rather new and only a few states have it. The number does seem to be growing, though, and it appears to be a good thing. Community property with right of survivorship (CPWROS) started in 2001 and is probably a better way to go with property ownership than other forms.

The one great advantage is that on the death of the first spouse, the property is passed to the surviving spouse with 100 percent ownership. The property is then given a stepped-up value and no taxes will be owed on the house. This works best when the first spouse desires that the surviving spouse receive the property with 100 percent ownership rights and no taxes.

Problems from a CPWROS can occur, however, from creditors. Since the surviving spouse now owns the property in its entirety, it could suffer. Also, in a CPWROS situation, the property becomes that of the surviving spouse, regardless of what may be in the will.

CASE STUDY: ESTATE PLAN FOR JOHN AND BETTY CASPER

By Robert "Rusty" Tweed and Sam Ledwitz

"According to probate records, at the time of his death, Elvis Presley's estate was valued at $10.2 million, of which only $2.8 million was distributed to his heirs after taxes; 73% was taken by the taxman."

CLASSIFIED CASE STUDIES™
directly from the experts

Estate planning has two primary objectives:

1. Minimize estate taxes in order to pass on as much as possible to your heirs, and

2. Control how your money is distributed at your death.

When John Casper retired at 65, he and his wife Betty (age 62) had accumulated an estimated $5.2 million in assets consisting of:

Their personal home, valued at approximately $1 million

CASE STUDY: ESTATE PLAN FOR JOHN AND BETTY CASPER

$3 million in rental properties, consisting of a $1 million office complex and $2 million in multifamily rentals

Rollover IRA assets of $520,000

Unqualified investment assets of $540,000

Cash equivalents of $200,000

Based on their current life style, they wanted to receive at least $150,000 annually in income from their assets during retirement, which could easily stretch 20 years or more. In addition, they wanted to make certain that when they die, their heirs would receive as much of their estate as possible. At the time John and Betty came to Tweed Financial Services, they had three married children and six grandchildren.

Our preliminary estate planning recommendations and rationale were as follows:

1. To avoid having their estate go through probate, they needed to set up an "ABC Living Trust" and have their assets titled in the trust's name, with the exception of their IRA assets. The "ABC Living Trust" properly preserves both John and Betty's federal death (estate) tax exemption — saving the children and grandchildren several hundred thousand dollars in death tax.

   Additionally, the "ABC Living Trust" holds the assets in a way that allows the assets to get a full step up in basis on assets such as stocks and real property. In short, at the first death the surviving spouse could sell without capital gains tax or start depreciating rental property all over again — saving thousands of dollars in income tax.

   Furthermore, the children inherit their respective shares in a generation-skipping tax (GST) trust. This protects each child from future ex-spouses, potential creditors, and potential estate tax.

   In most states, assets not in a living trust are subject to probate when an individual dies. Probate is a court-supervised process for transferring assets to the beneficiaries listed in one's will.

CASE STUDY: ESTATE PLAN FOR JOHN AND BETTY CASPER

With a living trust, assets are administered for John and Betty's benefit during their lifetime, and then transferred directly to their beneficiaries when they die, without going through probate. This passes assets onto the heirs much quicker and without expensive probate costs. Assets and their values also do not become public record, providing the family with greater privacy.

John and Betty were named trustees in charge of managing their trust's assets, with their oldest son as a successor trustee. As successor trustee, he would manage the trust's assets if John and Betty ever become unable or unwilling to do so or in the event of their deaths.

2. Designated beneficiaries for their retirement account assets were modified to have the spouse as the primary beneficiary and the three children as contingent beneficiaries. After both spouses pass away, the children would become the primary beneficiaries. The IRA would be split into thirds and each child would have their required minimum distribution, calculated individually on each child's respective life expectancy. This offers the potential to reduce minimum distribution requirements and extend the deferral period, "stretching" the IRA.

3. A $2 million life insurance policy was purchased under an irrevocable life insurance trust (ILIT) with the three children as beneficiaries and their oldest son as trustee. Each year, John and Betty can gift $24,000 per child to the trust to pay the premium for the insurance. This transaction is commonly referred to as a Crummy Provision and allows the whole policy to be outside the parents' estate.

4. Within the living trust, we had the clients sell their $2 million in multifamily units and purchase tenants-in-common (TIC) properties through several 1031 exchanges, which allowed them to defer capital gains taxes on the sale of the buildings. TIC assets get a 30 percent discount on valuation because of illiquidity, which drops the current taxable equity to $1.4 million on a death tax return. The TIC would provide regular rental income as well as depreciation tax

CASE STUDY: ESTATE PLAN FOR JOHN AND BETTY CASPER

credits. This also freed the Caspers from the day-to-day issues of property management and allowed them much more time for travel. Real estate investments incur various risks, including but not limited to: illiquidity, limited transferability, and variation in occupancy, which may negatively impact cash flow, and even cause a loss of principal. Real estate values may fluctuate based on economic and environmental factors and are generally illiquid.

5. A Family LLC was created to take ownership of the commercial office complex. This would allow John and Betty to gift each of their six grandchildren $24,000 in shares in the LLC each year, effectively transferring ownership to their grandchildren and within seven years removing the commercial property from their estate. Income from the LLC could be used for their grandchildren's education and other expenses. TIC investments provide simplicity by eliminating active property management headaches. However, the owners do not have direct say over the day-to-day property management situations; they vote on major issues.

The overall impact of these actions eliminated probate costs when John and Betty die, began a planned migration of assets tax free from their estate to their children and grandchildren, reduced the taxable value of their assets, provided for the payment of eventual estate taxes through the life insurance policy, and left John and Betty with full control over their equity.

These situations and examples are presented for illustration purposes only; do not assume that the conclusions could be applied to any other person.

Robert "Rusty" Tweed is president and founder of Tweed Financial Services, Inc., an independent, comprehensive financial planning firm with offices in San Marino and Beverly Hills, California. Rusty is a registered rep with CapWest Securities Inc. Securities offered throughCapWest Securities Inc., Member FINRA, SIPC, MSRB. Tweed Financial Services and CapWest Securities Inc. are nonaffiliated. A Certified Estate Advisor® and prominent member of the Board of Advisors of the National Association of Financial and Estate Planners and the Tenants-in-Common Association, Rusty has assisted more than 600 clients to set up appropriate trust

CASE STUDY: ESTATE PLAN FOR JOHN AND BETTY CASPER

structures and has settled more than 40 estates. As a specialist in retirement investment planning, he manages in excess of $100 million for clients in the Los Angeles basin area, utilizing individual portfolios, managed equity accounts, real estate investment trusts, tenants-in-common offerings, real estate limited liability corporations, and private trusts.

Samuel B. Ledwitz, J.D., LL.M. (Estate Planning)

Bezaire, Ledwitz & Associates, APC

970 West 190th Street, Suite 275

Torrance, CA 90502

Tel: 310-769-4783

Fax: 310-769-4776

samuel@blalawfirm.com

19
Life Insurance

Although life insurance trusts have already been discussed, there are other ways that you might be able to use them in your planning.

Life insurance has many different uses. Part of your usage may be determined by your assets, such as whether your total assets are greater than your estate tax exemption. If they are not, then you do not need to be concerned about how or where the proceeds from a life insurance policy go. If they are large enough to be concerned about, then consultation with an estate planner will be needed.

Uses for Life Insurance

Here are a few ways life insurance can help those you leave behind.

Provide for the Needs of Surviving Family Members

This can be one of the most important purposes of life insurance, if there is this need for it. In fact, this could be one of the best ways to make funds available to the remaining family members, because insurance proceeds are usually given rather quickly. In some cases, however, it can take months, depending on the company.

While the estate is being settled, which often takes from six months to about three years, life insurance benefits can enable your family members to continue enjoying their present life style. It will also provide a monthly maintenance until the rest of the estate can be settled.

Pay for Immediate Needs and Bills

Other expenses will quickly be incurred around the time of your death, including possible medical and funeral costs. These can be high, and your family will appreciate having them covered by life insurance.

Estate taxes will also need to be paid before the estate is settled. If you have this money come from a life insurance policy, it may prevent the property from having to be sold in order to pay it. This could ensure that the property stays in the hands of the surviving spouse.

Debts that were left intact could also be paid from the settlement of a life insurance policy. This could ensure that creditors do not call shortly after the death of a loved one. Covering all remaining bills is a good way to allow remaining family members to continue on with their lives.

Create an Estate

Since a life insurance policy can generate a large amount of money from a little, it is the ideal tool to create an estate for your loved ones. This works well even if you do not have much money while you are alive. Insurance premiums are low, depending on how much insurance you want to buy.

You will need to decide whether to buy term life or whole life insurance. Which one you buy will probably be based on your needs. Term life insurance is far cheaper but needs to be paid each month in order to keep the policy in force. It will enable you to buy much more coverage for a smaller price tag. Whole life insurance, on the other hand, does cost more, but also has a built-in savings plan, which you can tap into if needed.

One definite advantage of a whole life policy is a possible paid-up feature. Once you have paid premiums for so many years, the interest builds up to give you enough to pay for the premiums each month. This can free up some of your money a few years down the road, and still keep your life insurance policy going.

Whether you place your policy's assets into a trust is up to you. You can name more than one beneficiary if you want, and the life insurance company will disburse it equally.

Equalize Gifts Among Children

If you have a farm or another piece of property that needs to stay intact, you can will that property to one of your children and use life insurance to create an equal value gift for the other children. This way, land for a farm or other business does not need to be divided, and the other children simply receive life insurance proceeds, keeping everyone happy.

Provide a Retirement Income

Cash values built into a whole life policy can be "borrowed" against the policy and used to provide an income upon retirement. This can be done while the owner of the policy is alive, but it will reduce the face value of the life insurance by the amount borrowed. You will need to borrow a lump sum and possibly place it in a bank account where you can receive higher interest than you can from the life insurance company. You can draw out the money as needed.

Enable a Business to Continue

If you have a business that is largely formed around you, then you need to have insurance to cover what could be serious losses to the business when you die. Other key people may be crucial to the survival of the business as well, and you may need insurance to cover losses caused by their deaths, as well. This could include people who are the inventors or developers of your products.

Business owners need to realize that when they pass away, the whole family could suffer great loss if the business is the only source of income. A good insurance policy could enable business debts to be paid and provide for the family.

Concerns About Life Insurance

Before you buy life insurance, it is important that you consider more than how much you need or want to get. Here are a few other things you need to consider.

The first thing you need to consider is, if you buy term, it will usually be for a term of about five, ten, or twelve years. This means that you are locked in for that long, and then you must reapply. If you should be in poor health at the time of renewal, your health insurance could become very costly, and you may not be able to get it anywhere else. You can usually get what is called guaranteed renewability, but the price is not guaranteed. The new price is dependent on your health and the age you have reached when you renew it.

This rise in price every so many years (at renewal time) means that eventually, it could become unaffordable. At some point, you will need to convert to a whole life policy. This will reduce your coverage, but you will not have any cash value for a few more years.

In some cases, it may be better just to start out with whole life. This is especially true if you want to build up a policy that pays for itself quickly. Although the insurance coverage you receive per dollar spent is much lower, the savings you could have once it reaches the point where it starts paying its own premiums could be well worth it. At that time, you could invest the difference somewhere else where much higher interest could be earned, and you could still have the life insurance. The premiums on whole life insurance never change, either.

20
Long-Term Care

The need for long-term care is probably more important than ever. Thanks to modern medicine, Americans are living longer than before. This means that there is a greater likelihood that a nursing home may be needed, especially since American families also need to work more than before. Husbands and wives often work away from the home, leaving no one at home to watch out for the elderly and take care of their needs.

As the need for nursing home care has increased, so have the costs that surround it. With longer life has also come a greater need for healthcare, as the body and mind now experience greater effects of aging. What has happened is that life continues to go on considerably beyond retirement years — sometimes 20 or more years longer then in the past. This means that the effects of aging are even greater and that health costs are also that much greater, especially since healthcare often must be done in a nursing home.

During that same amount of time, inflation has more than caught up with the savings of many people, and they find that they are coming up short of being able to provide for their needs. At a mere 4 percent inflation over a period of 20 years, for every dollar you had to start with, it will now cost $2.19; with 6 percent inflation, it will now take $3.21

to pay for the same thing. Buying power becomes less with each passing year, and inflation rates change every year. This shows that inflation needs to be a consideration when calculating your estate plan.

Other problems may come with having too much money. When you apply for Medicaid, they will require that you be nearly penniless in order to qualify. Estate planning will be needed to protect the assets you do have so that they are not totally destroyed. This was discussed previously in Chapter 17, "Health Needs."

Many are focused on the matter of estate planning, but there also needs to be a focus on potential long-term care. Many senior citizens have their needs provided for at home, but around 40 percent of those over 65 will need nursing home care at some time. It is possible that many people will live in a nursing home for years.

Long-term care covers many different needs and may involve treatment for the following:

- Alzheimer's disease

- Chronic illness

- Infirmity

- Terminal conditions

Treatment is available for those in nursing homes or assisted living situations, and can provide care for many needs, including the following:

- Daily care in bathing and dressing

- Eating and daily nutrition

- Supervised and skilled medical care

- Social needs

- Respite care

- Using the bathroom

- Recovering from an illness

- Pain management

- Help meeting doctor's appointments

- Getting medicine regularly

- Managing money

- Laundry

The list could contain many more things. It is even longer when care is provided for at home.

Two types of care are needed when it comes to long-term care, and both are generally covered by most long-term health plans. These are skilled care and custodial care. Skilled care involves treatment from a medical professional. Custodial care includes those services that do not require a professional. While these services can sometimes cross over, and the lines may seem to become distorted, they remain clear to the government.

When there is an injury or an illness that requires hospitalization, Medicare pays for this. After the patient is sent home and needs time to recover, Medicare will cover this also. That is about where Medicare help ends. This coverage is limited to about 60 days. This seems to work as long as there is some evidence of recovery. If it is decided, however, that the patient is terminal or needs long-term care, then this comes under a different category and Medicare most likely will no longer cover it.

Long-Term Care in the Home

Most of America's elderly are being given long-term care at home. This amounts to about 80 to 85 percent of the elderly in our land. These may require various degrees of care.

Most healthcare plans, especially the government-sponsored ones, will only provide financial help if the recipient has little income and almost no assets. This makes it necessary to remove most assets in order to get help from the government. Beyond the financial needs, however, there must also be a need for professional care. For those activities where care is needed such as bathing, changing diapers, feeding, and other such activities, but not professional medical help, the government will not provide for this; these are considered custodial care.

Besides Medicaid, there are other local agencies that can provide services and other small amounts of financial help.

Possible Equipment Needed for Care at Home

Before care in the home can be given, it is necessary to consider what costs may be involved in getting the home ready. Sometimes, home care may require modifications in the home itself before the home becomes usable to someone needing home care. These modifications may include:

- Access ramps

- Installation of lifts and ramps

- Wider doors and door frames

- Tub and toilet modifications

Besides these changes in the home, there may also be a need for some equipment. This could include things like:

- Wheelchairs

- Hospital beds

- Oxygen equipment

- Scooters

- Walkers

Financial Help May Be Available

Ideally, this equipment may not be needed. It is reasonable to assume, however, that if life continues, at least some of it will become necessary, and someone will need to pay for it. About half of those who reach 80 will need healthcare of some kind on a regular basis.

Most of those who care for their parents at home cannot do it entirely by themselves. Many hours may need to be spent as caregivers, for which there is no pay and often little financial assistance. Numerous people can be brought in to perform various services, which may cost anywhere from $10 to $25 an hour, on average. Because most of this will be custodial care and not skilled care, most of it falls financially on either the recipient or on those providing the care.

In very recent years, Congress seems to have become aware of what has been happening in the realm of long-term care being performed at home. This has resulted in a little loosening of the governmental wallet. This new help comes from various local agencies and may include financial help with necessities such as:

- Modifications of the home

- Utilities

- Rent

- Transportation

- Home repairs

- Legal help

- Counseling

Adult Day Care

Providing your loved one with adult day care could be a good alternative to nursing home care. These day care centers are generally open only on weekdays, from the morning until the time that most people get home from work. This means that you could drop off your loved one in the morning (if you work) and then pick him or her up in the evening. Some of these centers can also provide pick-up and drop-off services.

These centers have a variety of programs, and will usually include a lunch and possibly a snack in the afternoon. Some of the newer adult day care centers provide a range of medical services, too, so the recipient can receive some medical care or supervision if that is required.

A nice feature about adult day care centers is that Medicaid may pay for it, and so will many long-term care insurance policies. Although it is still in the experimental stage, Medicaid is paying for this service because it knows that this is a cheaper way to go than paying for nursing home care. It could help you with long-term care alternatives.

Respite Help Available

One of the biggest problems associated with home healthcare is the need of those who give care to be able to find some relief themselves. A local agency may have some people available who can help you with this. There are people who will come for a few hours, free of charge, and provide you with some time to get away for some needed personal refreshment and relaxation. This service is available regardless of the caregiver's income or assets.

Other options may be available, too. For instance, you often can get free meals delivered through services like Meals on Wheels. Senior centers may also provide meals and could provide some help by providing some relief and time away. Take the loved one to the center for a few hours — you could even do this on a regularly scheduled day of each week to cut down on your stress levels.

Long-Term Care Insurance

All of these expenses show the need for you to have long-term care insurance. It would cover many, if not most, financial needs connected with long-term care. Things like home modifications, medical expenses, home health services, and even someone to replace your caregiver for a few hours from time to time are included in some of these policies.

The need is there for a long-term care addition to your healthcare insurance policy while you have the assets. Look over a number of policies before any decisions are made, however, and be sure to check on the reliability of the company offering it. It is also very important to note what services are and are not provided.

Long-Term Care for Veterans

The Veterans Administration will provide services similar to those of Medicare. After an accident or an illness, they will provide nursing home care during recovery and some home healthcare, too. Although they may be more plentiful in their services than Medicare, they will not provide overall long-term heath care.

Hospice Care

Near the end of one's life, it is possible to receive specialized care. This includes pain care, comfort care, and just about anything else that may be needed in terms of care and equipment. Since 1982, hospice care can be included in your Medicare benefits. This Medicare program will cover most of the expenses in this situation. There is a degree of flexibility in the various types of care that are offered, including some in the way that various cultures treat those who are dying.

Hospice care typically starts once it has been medically determined that a person has six months or less to live. Entering into a hospice situation, you will find that there are many services that are provided during this time to meet daily needs. This includes regular handling of sanitary needs, eating, care, social needs, as well as helping the family to know what to do and how to provide the best level of care during this time in the patient's life.

Hospice care covers the needs of those who may be dying from just about any kind of disease. The care will not eliminate the care from the family. Instead, hospice care is designed to work with the family and help them care for their loved one in his or her last days. This means that teams are available to instruct family members on how they can best provide some of that care.

When a family has a loved one who comes to that point in his or her life, it may be important for them to seek help in providing the right kind of care. The family may decide to try to do this themselves in order to keep the loved one nearby, but this often results in extreme stress, as well as putting one in a position of doing things for which they have no expertise or knowledge. Putting that loved one in a hospice care center relieves much of that stress. It also places the loved one into the hands of professionals and provides pain medications to make them comfortable in their last hours.

Planning for Long-Term Care

Most likely, many Americans will need some kind of long-term care. This book has shown how it can be very expensive and time-consuming for someone who is already working to provide this kind of care for a loved one. The good thing is that there are a number of options, both financially and provisionally, for meeting those needs. You need to develop a plan that will meet those needs.

In your planning, however, you cannot know the future. While you still have control of your assets, it becomes important that you talk with an estate planner and health insurance agent to:

- Discover what options are available

- Understand the proper timing in your planning

- Know what government programs are available and what they require

- Provide for those needs in the best possible way

- Present to your children what your interests are

There are many Americans with no plan for potential long-term care needs. With Americans now living longer, and sometimes without the benefit of good health, it is imperative that you have a good plan. Provide for the possibility and help your loved ones get the help they may need to provide for you.

Section V

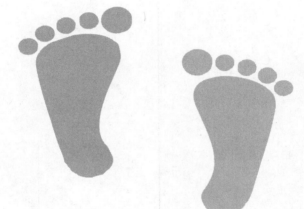

Putting the Vision to Work Through the Years

21
Making Changes

After you decide upon your vision, and you have the necessary groundwork in place, you will need to be able to make some changes as time moves on. Time often brings the unexpected, and it can bring those unexpected things at a time when we need or want them the least.

The ability to make changes to your estate planning documents means that you need to plan the instruments of your vision with a degree of flexibility built into them and an ease to be able to make those changes when needed. Of course, some instruments cannot be changed after you implement them. This means that you should not put all your assets into that single basket. Even in those instruments, however, great care needs to be given to be able to foresee as many possible future trouble spots as you can.

You should be aware that there is no such thing as a perfect arrangement when it comes to estate planning. Some situations may come close when they are created, but everything else around it can change, creating the need for more changes.

After your estate plan has gone into operation, it is time to watch over those plans. It is not a time to relax, believing that all will be well the rest of your days. Here are some reasons why changes may be needed.

Reasons for Possible Changes

There are many reasons why you should keep an eye on your estate planning tools. Time changes a lot of things. Here are a few reasons to help you understand the importance of watching to make sure that everything is as protected as it should be — and that it stays that way.

Your Understanding Changes

Since most people rely on someone else to do their estate planning for them, there may be a limited amount of understanding when the plan is implemented. For instance, your estate planner, although experienced, may not fully understand all the possibilities that are available to you. He or she may have focused almost entirely on a few options and may not know of some recent possibilities that might suit your needs better.

After some time elapses, this planner may discover that another tool may be better able to accomplish your needs than the ones you are using. An example of this might be the unitrust. Many people who create a trust find that this new instrument may provide the greater level of flexibility that they have been looking for. At this time, however, not all states permit it. You should know that probably most estate planners do not know all options and that you are somewhat at their mercy when it comes to what options are on the table.

This is why you need to become educated about estate planning. This will enable you to ask intelligent questions about other possibilities, should those options not be mentioned.

Remember that you are paying a good amount to obtain the services of an experienced estate planner, and you should get the best plan for your money. Do not count entirely on the knowledge of the estate planner and leave the decisions to him or her.

You may also forget about all the things that are in your estate plan after a while and may need to pull it out every now and then to review it. As you do so, you may decide that it is now inadequate for what your vision needs to accomplish. Changes may need to be made to ensure a better fulfillment of your plan.

The Laws Change

This could easily be one of the largest reasons for making changes to your estate plan. Tax laws, and other ones, too, change all the time.

For you, this means that a perfectly drawn-up plan may have been excellent yesterday, but today it will no longer do. This could create a need to adjust your plan from time to time. It is a very good idea to review your plan once a year with your estate planner — or on your own, if you created your own plan — and make sure that new laws are taken into consideration. If you have drawn up your own plans, it is recommended that you find an estate planner who is familiar with current laws and have them review your estate planning arrangements. He or she would keep up on these laws for their clients. Besides, you probably do not want to have to try to understand all the changing legalities. Hire a professional and save some time.

Remember that the IRS especially watches over certain types of structures. If they find an incorrectly formed organization or operation of that structure, then they could discount it altogether, suddenly leaving you to pay a large amount of taxes. Of course, your option could be to go to court and fight the decision of the IRS. It probably would be cheaper, however, just to bring in a qualified estate planner who can help you to keep one step ahead and prepared to meet the legal changes as they come along.

Your Situation Changes

Your situation could change. This happens all the time when the unforeseen, or the thing least wanted, becomes part of your life. Things you had hoped would not happen sometimes do.

The unexpected could include:

- Spouse dies first

- Divorce

- Beneficiaries die

- Remarriage

- Children marry greedy mate

- Hospitalization

- Long and expensive illnesses

- Estate lost due to some negligence

- Lawsuits

Whatever the plan, something can go wrong. For this reason, it is a very good idea not to use an estate plan that has only irreversible components in it. While one or two elements may be irreversible, you should have other elements that will allow you to make changes to them, as needed.

This is to make sure that all of your eggs are not in one basket. Your assets are better protected, as well as your needs for an uncertain future, with some flexibility in your plan.

An example of this would be if you irreversibly place all of your assets into a trust for your spouse. You had an understanding that the estate would be used for the spouse's maintenance, and some would go to the children also when you die. The balance would then be given to the children when the surviving spouse dies. A divorce comes along and the spouse gets remarried and has more children. If your estate planning instruments are irreversible, no changes can be made, and it is doubtful that all of the estate will go where you intended.

One option here is to allow a trustee to make some changes. This would depend on who the trustee is, or who may be called upon to replace that trustee if he or she should die earlier than expected. Other expectations of the funds and what is to happen to them will need to be spelled out in the documents that create your trust or other instrument.

Your Needs Change

When you created your estate plan, it only made sense that you created it to meet your needs at the time. Time has passed and you have some new needs now. Medical bills may have come along, there are new grandchildren, some grandkids could use some help with school bills, or a son wants a loan to start a business, and other new things.

Another realistic possibility is that your assets will change for the better. You had a relative pass away and you were left in the will. Now you have many more assets, and will need to include them in your estate plan so your estate will not get eaten up with taxes. This could create new possibilities for you, and you may need to create a new estate planning instrument to control the new assets.

Another important possibility that you need to think about is preparing to qualify for Medicaid if you or your spouse should need it, and not having to lose your estate to do it. This requires advance planning of at least five years. Any money that is placed into a trust up to five years before applying for Medicaid is considered part of your estate and could delay your being accepted into the program. See the chapter dealing with qualifying for Medicaid (Chapter 13, regarding trusts).

Your Plans Change

Your original goals have now changed, and you want to bring your plan up to date to match the new ones. This will require some modifications. Possibly, a son has proven that he is not able to control large amounts of money, and now you need to make changes that will help him to be able to use the money, with supervision and in a limited way. This may mean that you take the money out of one instrument and create another just for the purpose.

Other things can change, too, such as the naming of a trustee, adding of beneficiaries, changing of guardians or executors, and more. Many people, although they created a fine estate plan, create unnecessary problems by not keeping their plans up to date. This can cause chaos and unintended problems if there have been accidents that have left heirs disabled and in need of long-term care, beneficiaries who are deceased, divorces that have occurred, and other unexpected situations.

The Tools Change

When you created your estate plan, you may have chosen to use the best instrument available at the time. Since then, however, a brand-new instrument has come along that would better enable you to accomplish your vision for the future of your heirs.

This new instrument may provide you with better tax options, greater flexibility, or greater control over the assets after you are gone, helping to ensure that your future generations will get some of your estate as well. Another thing that could happen is that the IRS may no longer recognize an instrument you had chosen earlier. For example, this could occur with FLPs, since so many people are trying to misuse them.

Your Location Changes

When you move, especially if it is to a new state, the laws that affect your estate planning instruments may also change. You can only know whether they do by consulting with an estate planner in your new location. Some instruments, especially if they control assets in another state, you may want to leave alone, because they may be in perfect agreement with the laws there.

Assets in the new state, though, may need new planning measures and the creation of new instruments to accomplish your plans in the new place. One example would be the percentage of assets you need to leave to your wife. In some states, it may not matter, but in others, you could be required to leave up to half of your estate to your spouse, and some for your children, depending on their ages.

Estate Planning With Flexibility Built In

The idea of flexibility means that you have the power to make changes— or that someone else does — if they should be needed. Many people, however, can put a larger portion of their estate into various estate planning instruments for tax reduction in such a way that few changes may need to be made.

One of these instruments would be an irrevocable life insurance trust

(ILIT). Since multiple beneficiaries can be named on the trust, as well as alternates, there should not be a problem with this type of device. The only major decision would be how much to put into it and how much to leave behind for possible needs of the future. You do need to remember that any ILIT cannot be undone once it is created — if it is to be a valid tax-saving instrument.

Flexibility in your plan should be arranged in such a way that changes to it can be made without having to pay some kind of expensive fee every single time. If that is not possible, then efforts should be made to keep the costs as low as possible.

When it comes time to make a change to your will, for instance, it is simpler to add a codicil rather than to rewrite the whole document. Major changes, of course, will demand the rewriting of the whole document, but by careful planning in the first place, this may not be necessary.

Some changes can be easily made at convenient (and possibly predictable) times. These may include:

- Naming contingent beneficiaries

- Naming trustees (plural, if desired)

- Naming trustees (third-party)

- Naming executors

Things like births and deaths, divorces, or people falling out of favor with you will make it necessary and unavoidable, at times. However, with some instruments, such as payable-on-death bank accounts, life insurance, and some other estate planning instruments, changing some of these things can be achieved without any costs involved.

This shows another advantage of using more than one type of instrument in your planning. Other methods can also be low cost, if you are concerned about this.

Flexibility also needs to be added due to upcoming changes in estate laws (in 2010). The size of an estate that is taxable will change starting in 2011. That is, unless Congress passes new laws that will set up new amounts for how much passes tax free when there is a death. If there are no new laws passed, then things will continue on as they were in 2001. This means that only $1 million in assets will be tax free per person, and estate tax will once again be collected at a rate of 55 percent.

It certainly is not too early to be aware of what is going on in Congress and state legislatures. Instead of waiting until the last minute, you may want to talk with your estate planner in advance, just in case.

You do not want to get caught in a long line of clients rushing around at the last minute to make massive changes to their estate planning methodology. Much of what you are going to do should be simply to put your additional assets into several instruments designed to reduce your taxes. Do not be in such a hurry at that time, however, that you make mistakes simply because the deadline catches you unprepared. At best, however, members of Congress have good reason to want to pass the needed new legislation — they have estates, too.

Keeping the Changes as Simple as Possible

Proper estate planning does not mean that everything has to be complicated. Although precise wording and careful planning is needed, which is why you are better off using an experienced estate planner, some estate plans can be modified without too much difficulty.

An attorney will be needed in most cases to ensure that the right procedure has been followed and that the additions or changes are valid. In most cases, most of your assets will need to have been distributed to the various instruments, depending on the ones you have used.

22
Preparing the Beneficiaries

Depending on the amount of wealth you have, and how far into the future your vision extends, it is essential to prepare your beneficiaries properly. It is only by proper preparation that your vision can be fulfilled.

This requires that a planned strategy be designed and then carefully executed. However, the plan, for obvious reasons, will stop after the first succeeding generation unless your vision and the tools to carry it out are passed on with the wealth.

This makes it necessary to have a vision in place with workable tools so that you can start preparing the heirs early in life — at least early enough that they will still be teachable. Here is where you will find the difference between merely leaving an inheritance and leaving behind a powerful legacy with people capable of making it last for generations to come. Of course, this kind of legacy will require a large amount of wealth from the start and a plan while your children are still at home.

Although some of this has been mentioned in an earlier chapter, other aspects will be looked at here. Some lessons that need to be passed on, if the wealth is going to last, are:

- Values first

- A strong work ethic

- An appreciation of money

- A family pride

- A public purpose

- A sense of preparing for the future

- Desire to continue those values

- Accountability

- Desire to do your best

- Stewardship that manages for others' good

- Teachability

Although other values could be passed on, it is important that these values be at the top of the list. Without these, it is unlikely that wealth will last very long.

Here are some details about each of the above issues.

Teaching Values

Values, in our modern society, are often all but forgotten. People are looking for shortcuts to get to the top, and it sometimes seems that values can be forgotten in the process. As a result, wealth is too often associated with people who have little character. The kind of character that will enable your son or daughter to adequately control, dispense, and build wealth, however, does not fit into that type of personality.

The values that have already been mentioned, such as a strong work ethic, a public purpose (as opposed to a selfish one), and a desire to pass those same values on to successive generations, can be supported by regular attendance at a church, or through other religious groups. By having a church background, the children can have these worthy values instilled in them from the start, and reinforced throughout their lives. It is also attached to a higher authority in that case, making these great values ever stronger not only in their minds, but also in their future homes, which will help encourage these values to continue on a multigenerational level.

Values are the first pillar in these valuable lessons, simply because they must be the foundation upon which the others can comfortably lie. Without the right foundation, there will be no reason why the rest of the values should be kept and practiced, let alone perpetuated on to the children.

The following is a brief explanation of each of these values that need to be communicated to your heirs if your assets are to be used wisely, and last for more than one or two generations.

A Strong Work Ethic

You may have heard of wealth simply ruining those who received it. Money can make a person:

- Lazy

- Good for nothing

- Indifferent to others

- Selfish

Although this does not always happen, everyone has heard about some spoiled rich kid who is good for nothing, and unless you want that stereotype on your future family members, you will need to teach some real values.

The one thing that will probably save the day when wealth is transferred to your heirs is the values that they already possess. If they have already learned the value of work and the joy of personal achievement, then that attitude will probably continue. If, however, they have never learned this and have not developed a good work ethic, then money will probably do more harm than good in the long run.

A good work ethic is usually taught by a combination of four things:

- Seeing a good and consistent example in those they respect

- Being made responsible at an early age

- Learning the value of work through personal accomplishments

- Having to earn spending money and not being handed it every time it is asked for

A Genuine Appreciation of Money

When a child is given money simply for the asking, he or she tends to take it for granted. This idea can only lead to trouble, because then the child does not see the value in working to earn more and replace spent money, nor will they see the value in carefully spending it or accounting for it. This attitude can only generate a carefree "spend it today" attitude, a life of living only for the moment.

When children have to earn their money, and then can spend only what they earn (at least much of the time), they learn to watch it carefully and place a greater value on it. They learn that it does not come easily, thus creating watchfulness that also leads to making wiser choices as to how to spend it in the best way.

Some children will always catch on to these ideas faster than others. Other children are always trying to borrow money from their siblings; they learn fast which ones know how to save and which ones never have any money. When they get old enough, you can teach them how to account for their money. Teach them:

- How to record their expenditures

- How to set up a percentage for savings with short-term and long-term goals

- To set aside a percentage for giving to others — to buy gifts, help worthwhile causes, for Christmas savings, and more

Once accuracy and recording of all expenditures is learned, you may even want to reward them more for keeping the records up to date. This teaches them that good recordkeeping is worthwhile.

A Family Pride

Regular family activities can help to develop a sense of closeness and pride in the family as a whole. Pride in the family should also be taught and encouraged, as well as a concern for the welfare of it. If done properly and consistently, this can create a unity and a closeness that can last through the years.

These activities should involve every member of the family and should be fun, varied, and in different places. It needs to build memories of good times. The values will then be associated with good memories, togetherness, and fun. Those values will be looked upon, if reinforced and pointed out from time to time, as being a key in family unity and good times. The children then will want to pass both of these on to their children.

This unity, when coupled with values, will enable each family member to learn to be concerned for others. It will then help them to develop a sense of stewardship when the assets of the family (or part of them) are placed in their hands later. A concern for each other will naturally be extended toward a concern for those of the future who are also going to be in the family.

A Public Purpose

This one may be a little harder to teach, but it can be taught easier if started early. Many people who have amassed much wealth in the past (e.g., Rothschilds and Rockefellers) and in the present (e.g., Bill Gates) have learned that they can use their wealth to benefit others. Not only do they have the power to benefit others, but they have also learned to look at their wealth as making them responsible to use it to benefit others and society as a whole.

Rich people — including a number of movie stars recently — often take part in some program that will benefit some cause. They quickly learn that it gives a fulfilling sense of joy in knowing that their wealth can be used to further some cause that will benefit others. Once again, though, it needs to be taught from the earliest ages, so that children learn the joy that comes from giving, even just a little. If continued, it will help keep out a totally selfish view of their future wealth, and will help to develop lasting habits of benefiting others.

A Sense of Preparing for the Future

The children must also be taught to look at the assets under their control as an opportunity and a responsibility to help their own children and grandchildren. This means that the wealth cannot be seen as theirs alone, but as belonging to others as well. It will provide a key to future opportunities for those who will receive it.

Once a future view is established, then it is a simple matter of controlling it as a stewardship for the benefit of others. Care will then be taken for its preservation.

Desire to Continue Values

These values, if learned well, will so become a part of the young people that a deep conviction will lead them to want to pass those same values on to their children. They will understand that those values brought a certain added value with joy and purpose to them and that others can be "blessed" if they also develop those values.

This perpetuates not only those values that are being discussed here, but also provides their children with the values needed to perpetuate wealth. As you can see, these values form the foundation that will enable your vision for the use and perpetuation of your assets to future generations.

If these values are ever lost, and not perpetuated along with the wealth, then it will not be long before the wealth is gone. This places a greater responsibility on you to teach your children to also pass the values on along with the assets.

Accountability

Accountability always carries with it a difficult side. Some people are by nature very private, making it difficult for them to want to be accountable to anyone, even if the motives are entirely pure. Others may not want to take the time to have others review what they do with what they may consider to be theirs.

Accountability, however, is a great way to create a degree of precaution and safety. It helps people to be above reproach in their financial dealings and will also build confidence in their leadership and character. It is often when individuals no longer want accountability, or when they try to dodge it, that questions will arise that should call for immediate answers.

When creating a trust, or similar instrument, accountability should be demanded. This accountability should be demanded from:

- A trust agency, if used

- A trustee, no matter who

- A board of trustees — more than one

Accountability should apply to those instruments that control assets given to the use of the family as a whole, rather than assets distributed just to individuals. This will ensure the longevity of those assets and that they are used for the benefit of all involved, instead of for the good of one or two.

Accountability, and a willingness to allow oneself to be held accountable to others, is a good value that needs to be taught and then passed on. Along with these other values, it can ensure that the family as a whole is continually able to get a bird's-eye view of how the assets held for the family are being used and developed.

Do Your Best

Mediocrity should never be accepted. People of wealth have the same ability, and possibly a better education, to prepare them for significant achievement in their field of choice. Excellence, however, needs to be taught and encouraged, just as any other value. Doing your best should apply to everything that a young person does, not simply in those things that he or she enjoys the most.

Once young people have learned to give themselves to the task placed before them, they are then able to direct that "do your best" mentality to wherever it may be needed. This produces real character, and will enable them to focus on the best use of the assets under their control. This will also reduce waste and extravagance.

Stewardship That Manages for Others' Good

Looking at the assets received as a tool to bring benefit to others is probably a culmination of all the other forces at work. This attitude produces a cautionary view of all expenditures and makes decisions based on ultimate good rather than immediate want or the limited need of others.

This value can be communicated effectively only by having the student in close proximity to the teacher. One way to do this might be to give the young person a small account and actually let them manage it for someone else. Provide time for input, questions, and some instruction about why certain decisions may or may not be good in relation to the person whom the money is being managed for.

Teachability

Being able to receive advice, and not merely give it, can help children develop in the realm of financial wisdom. This means that they are able to receive counsel from others, including other family members, and are able to apply it to the situation.

Teachability only comes with a humble spirit that believes in the ability to learn something from others. Once individuals reach a point where they think they know it all and do not need counsel, mistakes may soon follow. Although even the best counsel could be wrong, being able to receive advice without developing a complex over it is maturity. Learning to ask for it when needed is even better.

23
Expanding the Assets of the Estate

Once the assets are placed into the hands of the heirs through trusts and other instruments, then it becomes their responsibility to ensure that the wealth of the family grows. This is only in those cases where the wealth of the family is sufficient to give personal wealth to the children and still have enough left over to have a separate wealth for the benefit of all the family members. Making this family wealth grow will certainly be a tough process, and not just any family member is up to the task. Without this needed work, the assets are most likely headed downhill. This wealth can be developed and built up to last for many generations.

Building the Wealth

Building this wealth will involve making sure that the family wealth is growing on as continual a basis as possible. In order to do this, it will need to be constantly overcoming several obstacles:

- Inflation

- Taxes

- Market fluctuations

- Fees

- Number of dispersals (added beneficiaries)

- Emergency lending

This task cannot be left in the hands of trust agencies, nor should it be left in the hands of only one family member unless he or she is a financial genius and above question in character. Accountability is needed here because assets may not be used to the best possible profit for the family as a whole.

Once slack or indifference develops, then atrophy and diminishing of the assets may result. This means that a regular review is needed with ways in place to determine expectations, needs, and projections. Also, some way to compare market events as a whole with specific schedules should also be considered. At times, the market will fluctuate and it will diminish some of the value of the estate, with little that can be done about it. The ability to measure, though, needs to be there so that it can be determined whether it is a market problem or a problem with the person managing the assets.

If the care of the trust assets is left in the hands of a trust company, then there needs to be a way to hire and fire companies, if necessary. Terms and expectations of the company should be clear in the way of reports and information needed. It is possible that some companies may not be so willing to cooperate with any extra paperwork, but it should be expected. Additional costs may be incurred for more detailed reporting.

Wise decisions will depend on things like performance data of the various instruments used for profit. Mutual funds, stocks, and other financial instruments will all need to be watched and considered in light of how other instruments are performing. Instead of letting one instrument sit with little profit, it should be moved to a higher-performing instrument if it shows promise of continuing to do so.

Choosing a financial advisor to gain expert counsel is a good idea. This could also mean that new options could become available to the family. How he or she performs, presents data, and considers possible new markets for investment should determine his or her usefulness — and whether it is time to hire someone else.

Family members who have the task of seeing to it that there is a profit will need to handle several tough areas, possibly all at the same time. These will include:

- Uniting family members who think differently and may have different goals

- Ensuring selected financial advisors are reliable and performing as expected

- Ensuring a wide diversification for a safer control of investment assets

- Tapping into family members' areas of expertise

- Presenting usable information at regularly scheduled family meetings

When some of the assets of a family are together, possibly under a trust, then there are several ways that the assets can benefit both the estate and the beneficiaries. A large sum will be needed, however, for this type of situation. When the above characteristics are operational within a family, then there can be a unified strategy around which the family members and their spouses can work and benefit.

This unity of mind and effort toward the accomplishment of preserving family assets for future generations will prevent the assets from needing to be distributed, and they can be perpetuated for a long time in this form. Of course, the trust itself controls the assets, and this is governed by the way that the founder of the trust established the operation and appointed means for the distribution of assets and income.

It will largely be up to the individual family members to take it upon themselves to not only benefit from the assets coming to them, but to manage the estate to the best interest of all involved. It is up to individual family leaders and appointed individuals to continue the vision of what the family wealth can do for future generations, not just the present one.

The Family "Bank"

Many families create a family bank when there is wealth to be passed on from one generation to the next. This not only provides for the wealth to be protected, it also makes the wealth available to family members who may have a need for it.

This is also where several family members who have financial ability and knowledge, as well as the values needed, provide the necessary protection over the family's assets. Money can be loaned out as needed, and assets or distributions can also be made from it.

Many things can be done with a family bank once you have the right people in control. Input should also be possible from other family members, and needs or requests for loans from the family bank are each to be handled separately.

Incentives can be given for larger awards or loans when the loans are used properly (wisely) and repaid in due time. Conditions would also need to be laid out in advance of what kind of behavior would prevent loans in the future from the family bank being made to a family member.

All terms should be in writing before any money is loaned out so that there can be no accusations of favoritism or neglect. The key family members chosen by the family provide guidance, but the meetings should be open for other family members to attend. This is crucial so that the younger members who will eventually replace the older ones learn how the values, rules, terms, and other conditions apply.

Besides this, any applications for loans and all terms should be in writing so that there is not any money being passed "under the table." It could be a good idea for a third party to handle the loan aspect of the family bank.

Annual reports of all financial transactions of the family bank should be reported on paper and given to all members each year, or more frequently. It is not a good idea, however, to report to the family as a whole what each family member owes to the family bank. Neither should it be passed on in the reports, or by any other means, what the status is of any individual members. It should be left up to that family whether they want that information known.

Section VI

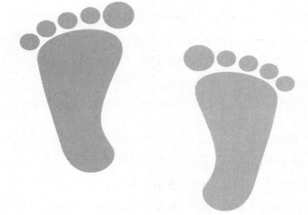

Forseeing Problems that Might Hinder the Fulfillment of Your Vision

There is no such thing as a vision for the future without possible opposition. As long as there are possibilities that many other people do experience, you will need to work to eliminate as many of them as you can. This requires that you pay attention to each of these areas, especially where it could pertain to your situation, and plan accordingly.

As you read this section, jot down on paper any potential problems that you foresee might be a problem in your case. Then take those concerns and thoroughly discuss them with your estate planner. Make sure that you leave that meeting confident that the problem has a solution worked out and that you are satisfied that the solution should work.

Your loved ones will appreciate your watching out for their interests — as well as their future — if you do take an extra step to protect those assets for them. And in most cases, they probably will not mind you taking a little larger portion of it for estate planning purposes in order to provide the protection your assets will need for their benefit.

You may wonder why you should not just leave it all in your will. If you do not have wealth that amounts to more than a couple of million dollars, then that could actually work for you. However, as it has been mentioned, there are problems with a simple will, one of them being that a will can be rather easily contested. You also should understand that problems are even more likely to happen if:

- There is someone you are not going to put in your will

- There are children from more than one marriage

- You are going to leave unequal portions to the beneficiaries

Estate planning and preparing for all contingencies is needed, in part, because of what happens to some people when they see the possibility of getting money and assets. This brings out the worst in some people. Families being destroyed with brothers and sisters never speaking to each other again, children ceasing to provide anything for the welfare of a surviving parent or stepparent, children of one family being totally neglected, and other horrible situations can occur. In many cases, these sometimes permanent problems can be averted simply by taking an extra step or two in preparation.

In most cases, it is the will of the originator of the wealth to pass that wealth on as simply as possible so that the children can also enjoy it, and the grandkids, too. Others, however, may look at it differently, and may be willing to enter into legal battles just to get a larger portion. If the planners of the estate could see what would happen after he or she is gone, they most likely would have taken the extra time to prepare against those problems. With that said, here are some things that may prevent your vision of passing your wealth on to your heirs from actually being carried out, and how to prevent some of them. You may notice that some of these issues have already been touched on in other chapters, but it will be looked at in a larger scenario in this section.

Other problems can arise if you simply do not prepare correctly, as often occurs on some do-it-yourself estate plans. Since you may not know all the laws that could affect your wealth transfers, it is possible that your whole estate plan may be counted as null and void. This could mean then that your estate will be divided up by the state you live in, and it could take years to actually be transferred to your heirs. Even worse, though, would be that it still might not go where you had planned.

24
Choosing the Beneficiaries

After you have your vision in mind and know what your ultimate goals are for your wealth in the lives of your children and grandchildren, you can select the beneficiaries. Your plan should be in writing by this time so that you can evaluate it from time to time, and effectively pass those ideas and values on to them, as well as your wealth.

The beneficiaries need to be selected according to your plan. You need to start by making a list of all of them, and then beside those names, write down:

- The assets to be given

- The provisions needed (as for a spouse or dependent child)

- The gifts (now, later, and after you die)

- The instrument to be used (e.g., trust, life insurance, or bank account)

- The responsibilities needing appointments (e.g., trustee and executor)

After you make up this list, you must make a list of any of your close relatives whom you definitely do not want to include among your beneficiaries. You must not forget about these names, so keep it on the same pages as the other names. You will definitely need to mention these people in your will. To learn more about this, see the chapter on wills.

Here are some basic assumptions that you should make as you prepare to name your beneficiaries. Even though you have already had a list in your mind for a long time, these are good guidelines to follow. If you differ from these ideas, you need to read on.

- Equal divisions for siblings

- Consideration of debt and gifts already received

- Special needs (as for a disabled child)

- Spouse not fiscally able

The following is a more detailed look at each of these things.

Equal Divisions for Siblings

Even if your children have been "perfect" during their time on earth, there is no telling what money or assets might do to change that and bring out anger, greed, or other feelings — and possibly actions to match. One way to ensure that there is as little trouble as possible would be to divide up equal shares with the siblings.

One example of a family that had real problems with unequal treatment would be young Joseph in the Bible. While his father loved him especially, his brothers came to hate him that much the more. They quickly became jealous because dear Dad treated him better and bestowed more attention and blessings on him. One day, when Dad was not around, they decided get rid of Joseph, so that their plight and problem — and jealousy — could be ended. Who knows what might happen when Dad (or Mom) is no longer there.

Your best policy would be to give equal portions to each one of your children, where possible. If you favor one because you believe that he or she has a "greater need," then it is possible that deep resentment could be created in the other children. By doing so, you may appear to be rewarding a lack of ability, rather than by giving equal shares to both those more successful and those who have been less successful.

As it has been mentioned in earlier parts of this book, a value can only be taught if there is a solid example of that value in the first place. If you teach family unity, and always seek the good of the family members as a whole, an unequal inheritance will teach something different. This type of situation has often divided families, and the siblings have never spoken to each other again.

Considerations of Debt and Gifts Already Received

Young people have odd memories. They can remember when you gave gifts, loans, or other favors toward a sibling. These memories might come into play when the reading of the will takes place.

Since you want your children to live in harmony with each other the rest of their days, you do not want your wealth to be the one thing that severs that relationship. If you have already given some gift or loan to one of your children and not to the others, you will want to even the score, if possible. This means adding or subtracting from the wealth already given and balancing it out so that it is equal to the others' total share.

If you feel that you need to know more about how they might feel in certain circumstances, then you might talk to them about it before your plans get set in print. This could either serve to reinforce your worst nightmare, or uphold your beliefs that they are understanding angels who love each other and trust their parents' decisions. You also may want to discuss it with each one privately to get a clearer understanding of how he or she feels. This could also be a good time to ask if there is anything special that he or she might want. You can name these items specifically in your will and designate who is to receive them.

Concerning debt that is still owed to the wealth creator, it will most likely be looked at as an early gift if it remains unpaid at the time of death. One easy way to prevent hard feelings for uneven distributions would be to treat it as a gift and forgive the balance at some specified time, if it appears that it cannot, or will not, be repaid. To other siblings, a loan that is unpaid at the time of death will appear to be a portion of his or her inherited estate. The remainder can then be divided up among the others.

Special Needs — Disability

Your estate planning tools will need to be reviewed and brought up to date every now and then, for as long as you are still around. Your own needs and the needs of others will change as time marches on.

Some children, however, may still have similar needs over the years, especially in the case of a mentally or physically disabled child. Others may not be able to handle their finances. In these cases, and others, you will need to make special provisions for him or her to get through life with the proper needs being fulfilled.

Another special situation could be that of a disabled spouse. Money would need to be set aside for his or her care, and it would need to be money given in such a way that other children could not take it away, such as in a bypass trust. If he or she would need to enter into a nursing home in the event of your death, then you would also need to be sure that any funds set aside for it are not going to get in the way of being able to receive Medicaid.

As discussed previously, a spouse getting ready to apply for Medicaid assistance will need to have the trust set up by his or her spouse for it not to count toward his or her assets. The trust will also need to be irrevocable, must be set up at least five years prior to application, and the surviving spouse cannot have any control over it.

Spouse Not Fiscally Able

When there is a spouse who is either not able or not willing to handle the estate and its necessary paperwork, there is a way around this as well. It may mean that the assets need to go into a trust for the spouse and a trustee be designated to disperse the assets as appointed.

This should be discussed in advance so that the assets of the estate are preserved as much as possible. Unwillingness to handle the necessary affairs of the estate could lead to chaos and lost revenue. Handling trust funds and ensuring that they are invested for the largest benefit is time consuming.

Placing the assets in a trust may be a good move, especially if he or she is willing to go along with it. This will help to ensure that the money goes to the children that it should (in the event of a remarriage), and also places the growth of the trust in knowledgeable hands — if you use a third-party organization.

The spouse may be unwilling to handle the finances partly because of feeling ill-equipped to handle the job. In many homes, only one spouse handles the financial affairs and makes investments, pays the bills, and other dealings, while the other stays in the dark as to the actual working details. If anything should happen to the fiscally responsible spouse, then the other is left unprepared. For this reason, both husbands and wives should be prepared with at least a basic knowledge of the family finances and how they work.

In a case where the surviving spouse is either unwilling or unable, a third party could be used as a trustee. It may be better if an organization handles this, because this agency could serve as an extra protection for the spouse so that children cannot take advantage and pressure him or her prematurely into distributing the inheritance to them.

It could also be a good idea that the spouse have some choice about making changes in the decisions of the trust company, or power to choose a new company if desired. This gives the spouse the final vote in case something is not as it ought to be.

If there is a likelihood of remarriage, then you may even put some stipulations in the trust that he or she is only to be supported as long as there is no remarriage. At that time, his or her support becomes dependent upon the new spouse, and the assets then pass to the children. This type of arrangement could be worked out with either spouse, if the husband and wife would prefer it.

25
Deciding About Complicated Relations

Some families today need to be very concerned about "complicated relations." This type of situation means that careful thought and planning may be needed in order to work through the potential problems in order to come up with a seemingly sound solution. The word "seemingly" is used here because there are no 100 percent foolproof solutions. In most cases, though, good and careful preparation will eliminate many problems.

Several types of situations will often create problems, and in most cases, you can see it coming. Here are a few of them:

- Children from multiple families and remarriage

- Children who want their inheritance now, but the spouse needs the house to live in

- A spouse who may not pass on assets to the right children

- Business partnerships

- Co-owned property

Children From Multiple Families and Remarriage

This is a rather prevalent problem today, as divorce and remarriage are touching more families. The problem is often deepened if the children are grown at the time of the new marriage and do not know the surviving spouse well. This can create serious rifts and ill feelings because the children may want their money and assets, but it falls under the control of the surviving spouse.

How this is handled depends on whether the surviving spouse has her own estate. Generally, her estate would go to her children, and her husband's estate would go to his children. However, this is a rather new solution, since it used to be impossible to ensure that this would happen. Not long ago, all states required that the assets of the first spouse to die would go to the surviving spouse — without conditions. This meant that the property became entirely the property of the remaining spouse, and then he or she was able to give it to whomever they wanted. Obviously, the children of the first-to-die spouses often never received any inheritance unless the surviving spouse was generous.

When there is a remarriage and children are involved from both spouses, then potential problems may ensue later. Remember that although all of the estate can be passed tax free to your spouse, he or she cannot give it tax free to your children. So, unless you divert some of the money — if you have more than the exclusion amount — into a trust or other estate planning instrument other than just a will, then there will be a sizable reduction in the estate when the surviving spouse dies.

Estate taxes, both state and federal, will need to be set aside in advance, or the property may need to be sold in order to pay those taxes. If possible, it is best to have this money set aside in advance so that the property does not have to be sold, unless that is your plan. Remember, though, that the taxes need to be paid within nine months of the death, and that property may not actually be sold for a long time, especially if real estate is not selling swiftly in your area.

One possible solution to this problem could be using life insurance. Life insurance can be purchased with a designated amount — a percentage of the estate would work best — for both tax needs and to balance portions to be given to each of the children. They can be named as equal beneficiaries on the policy or given separate policies. Remember that beneficiaries can be added, or taken away, at any time. This makes it an effective way to make your needed adjustments easily.

Further tax reductions can be obtained if the money from the life insurance is placed directly into a trust for the children. This money then bypasses the estate tax and much more money is kept in the estate, for which the children will be grateful.

Children Want Their Inheritance Now, but the Spouse Needs the House to Live In

Problems can arise if there is an impasse as to what should be done with the property when the assets are given to the spouse, either permanently or temporarily. It is a good idea to talk to your spouse in advance — remember that usually the woman is the survivor, statistically — and see what her thoughts may be. If she is determined to live in that same house until death, or a transition to a nursing home, then the likelihood of problems is even greater. A woman can typically live now somewhere between eight and fifteen years longer than her husband. The problems come because the children will often not want to wait until they are too old to really benefit from the wealth.

This creates a real impatience on the part of the children, who may not want to wait until she is gone to get what they feel should be theirs now. The only way you can really tell in advance is to get their thoughts on the matter before the estate planning is complete. Only you will know whether this is a good idea or whether you might not need to consult them. Sometimes, however, not consulting with them may cause more problems. They may be even more angered that they were not consulted in the first place.

If one or more of your children insist that they get their portion shortly after you die, then there could be legal trouble. Once again, a little prevention may be better than nothing at all. You may want to work toward a compromise. Here are some possible solutions.

- Place a portion of the estate into the children's hands at death, or before, as a gift. This should serve to take off some of the edge of feeling left out until it is too late.

- Let the spouse stay in the house for a limited time, say five to seven years, and then sell the house and obtain another one for him or her. The children would then get a portion, and the spouse would be taken care of, too. Other assets from the estate or sale of the house will need to be set up to provide maintenance for the spouse.

- Try to prevent children from suing for their portion by reminding them that legal fees are very high and that it would only serve to reduce the estate and could seriously, and possibly irreparably, damage family relationships.

- If the estate is too small to give an equal portion to the children, then the house will most likely need to be sold to bring about a resolution.

Spouse May Not Pass On Assets to the Right Children

When there is a concern that the surviving spouse may not pass the assets into the hands of your children, there is one thing you can do, depending on whether you have the money to do it.

All you need to do is to create a backup plan to create an inheritance for your children. You simply need to buy a life insurance policy for the heirs equal to the amount you intended to give them. Designate the children by name to be the beneficiaries and give instructions that the money is to be divided equally among them.

It is possible, though, that the fact that there is such a backup ready may further encourage the surviving spouse to not give any more assets to the children. But at least the children will still get an inheritance equal to the amount originally intended.

If you do go through with this plan, however, make sure that the funds needed to continue paying for the premiums are not left in the surviving spouse's hands, if there is the possibility that these funds may be diverted. Of course, the benefit would be lost in that case, unless the policies are self-paying (only whole life policies have this feature) by that time.

Business Partnerships

Business partnerships are another potential cause of conflict when one of the partners dies. The conflict is apt to be stronger if the business is struggling and the other partners are not able to buy off the partnership of the deceased. The result could be one of the following:

- All of the partnership investments could be lost

- The business could be sold off by force

- Family members could gain control of the corporation

There are two things that may be done here instead of taking a total loss. First, you could arrange that the partners make a sizable payment toward recovering your spouse's investment, then you could arrange for a payment plan to recover the balance.

Another thing that could be done to prevent the possibility of a total loss would be to purchase life insurance from the organization of the business for the value of the investment, plus interest. This ensures that the money is recoverable, and it would not take that much in the way of monthly payments to cover the amount of the investment. Since new business ventures always carry a large risk of failing, this would be a worthwhile investment to protect against personal loss in case the money is not otherwise recoverable.

Co-owned Property

Problems can also be expected if you leave property to more than one child — if they cannot get along well. While your intentions may be good and the property may be income producing, you may be setting up a situation where one could try to take the whole property from the other, just for peace of mind. And, for peace of mind, one may be willing to walk away from it.

Instead, if you really want to put both their names on it, it may be worth it to leave it in their hands for a while, but place it under the management of a third party, as in a trust. This way, the management decisions do not fall to the children, but the income and value of the property still belongs to both.

A better solution might be to see whether one of the children could buy out the other's share and then leave the property to that one. Or, get life insurance to create an equal value for any other children. If you do not have funds to create the life insurance, you may be better off, for the children's sake, to simply have the property sold on your death and divide the value of the property between them.

26
Preventing Unintended Divisions

The larger the estate, the more likely there will be people who want a share of it. It may be that they want a larger share than appointed, or they may want a piece of the pie but were left out of the estate plan altogether for one reason or another. In any case, when there are riches to be disbursed, people often will do what it takes to get to it. It is a good thing that there are courts, however, and laws in place that will help to greatly reduce such attempts.

The problem becomes much more difficult to solve, however, in the case of close relations, such as with a spouse or children of former marriages. The key is often as simple as ensuring that the wording of your will and other documents is just right, with which an experienced estate planner will be glad to help you. For some, however, it may take a little more foresight and planning.

Here are some areas where problems may arise:

- Children of the surviving spouse

- Children of the deceased spouse

- Uncaring children who think they deserves a larger portion of the estate

- One sibling who has been caretaker for some time

- A controlling stepparent

- A spouse of one of the children

- Children who just do not want to wait

- Parents who may use up the grandchildren's estate

Children of the Surviving Spouse

Children of a surviving spouse could easily be a problem with an estate, especially if the surviving spouse has any say over how the estate will be disbursed. What might happen is that the surviving spouse's children could encourage the spouse to give the money to them and leave the others out, since the others are not her children. Because the surviving spouse may already be in partial agreement with this plan, it is a good idea to prevent the possibility from the start. Even with the best of intentions, however, children can be very persuasive as adults and can put pressure on the spouse to change those intentions.

A bypass trust could be one excellent way around this. It will meet the needs of the surviving spouse and provide an income (all income goes to her) while she is alive. Then, after her death, the money and assets go to the children designated by the first-to-die spouse. This type of trust is ideal for this situation because it leaves no choices for the surviving spouse. She cannot alter the plan in any way, so pressure upon her would be no good. The children would have to wait, however, until her death.

Children of the Deceased Spouse

The children of the deceased spouse are the ones who would want the inheritance now rather than later. If there are not sufficient assets to provide for this, then they may push for the sale of the house so that the proceeds can be given to them. If the estate is large enough, life insurance can be purchased in advance for each of the deceased spouse's children. If the estate is too small, then the house may need to be sold, or some temporary agreement reached, until adequate housing and other needs can be met before the house is sold.

Problems are made larger if the spouse is determined to keep the house and live in it no matter what. This does sometimes happen. Sad to say, but this decision will probably cause the lawyers to be brought out if the children are determined to get their share. It is even more likely if the children do not know the surviving spouse very well.

Uncaring Children Who Think They Deserve a Larger Portion of the Estate

Every now and then, there is someone who simply thinks that he or she should have more than the others. While it is often a ploy simply to get a larger portion of the estate, someone with these intentions is often bold enough to work to get what he or she wants. This could definitely put the whole proceedings on hold and everyone will have to wait to get their share until it is resolved. Often, these types of claims can be dismissed, but they will have to be heard unless there are simply no grounds for the claim.

Grounds can be given for this type of claim if this son or daughter is doing some type of work around the home or family business and is not getting paid for it. If he or she is the only one doing it, then it could lead to resentment and a desire to get the accounts balanced after your death. This is one way to do it. If possible, try to offer some kind of payment for the work done, so that you eliminate both the need for repayment and the emotions that might fuel such a claim after you are gone.

Care should be taken (as has been mentioned earlier) to eliminate this type of claim as much as possible by giving each of your children the same amount. Be sure to take care of any personal loans beforehand and work to even out the total amount given before and after death. If there are uneven portions being distributed, then you could create the type of situation where the amounts given will be challenged. This is more likely to happen when the children are not close to each other, but it could happen in any family.

If you designate amounts to be distributed in dollars, this also could create an uneven distribution if the size of the estate fluctuates. It could leave one child with less than the other — or nothing — making someone potentially upset. It is probably better that you use percentages to designate an amount, such as 20 percent of assets, which will mean a more even distribution, no matter what happens to the estate over the years.

One Sibling Has Been Caretaker for Some Time

One person who often raises a problem in regard to desiring a larger portion is the child who may have been responsible for taking care of the surviving spouse (or both spouses). The likelihood of trouble is even more probable if the parents have to be helped or supervised for some time. Because this task is often unrewarding, and because he or she may often have to do it alone — brothers or sisters may live too far away — he or she may end up feeling that more is deserved, perhaps even all of the estate in some cases. Although some children feel an obligation to do this, and may not mind too much, some will do it only with an expectation of reward in mind.

The caretaker could be given a regular salary in order to alleviate this problem. If you think about it, if an agency were called in to provide home healthcare, they would have to be paid. If you elect to pay an agreeable salary to the child caretaker, then this should satisfy him or her who serves in this way. It will also make it more enjoyable for him or her to be involved, and will make it more fulfilling for them. Any other brothers and sisters should also be aware that pay is involved, too, in case the matter should ever come up again.

Without an immediate reward, however, the child may well have a legal right to make claims against a larger portion of the estate. This could be looked at as services that have not been recompensed, especially if he or she provides a detailed bill in relation to hours and possible other costs involved.

Controlling Stepparent

Once again, care should be taken if there is a potential for a stepparent to want control over all the assets and refuse to let them go. If the first spouse to die foresees that this may be a problem, then one solution is to simply give the assets directly to the children. This solves the matter once and for all, but only if the surviving stepparent has enough to live on.

Problems can be avoided here if the first spouse to die simply assumes that there could be a problem in this area. The truth is, even if a problem is not suspected, other influences, such as children of the stepparent, could change her mind, given enough time.

The will of the first to die can best be fulfilled if the spouses have separate estate plans, which should be done if there is wealth that is owned separately by each. This keeps matters clear and everyone knows where the boundaries are up front.

If the estate is tied up in the house, then life insurance can be purchased for each of the children. This way, each will receive his or her share and not have to wait until the stepparent dies and the house is sold.

Spouse of One of the Children

Many children have spouses who would just love to get their hands on the estate that is coming to their partner. Sometimes, this greed is so manifested before the death of the parent or stepparent that the person becomes obnoxious. Their intent is clear: they want the money as quickly as possible. Whatever their aspirations are for the money, you know it will most likely be used up quickly, and probably without the consent of the heir to whom it belongs.

Another potential problem, but related, is that you want the money to remain in the family if anything should ever happen to your daughter. She is married to a spouse who will certainly misuse it, and you are not certain that the marriage is stable enough to last through the years.

Protection can be obtained on the estate so that your daughter may only have limited use of the estate while she is alive, and then the money can be distributed directly to the children after she dies. Or wording can be put into the document that will even prevent the estate assets from falling into the husband's hands if she should die childless. In that case, the money would go to another brother or sister, or to their children. If there are no other ones, the estate can be designated to go to whomever you desire, or to some charitable organization.

This can be accomplished in one of two ways. The first is to put the money into a trust and make the children the beneficiaries. The daughter can serve as the trustee with access to profits from the trust, but not be allowed to remove any assets apart from specific guidelines. Better yet, a third-party trust company or bank can be the trustee who will watch over the assets even better.

Another approach to keeping the assets out of the hands of those you do not want to get them is to commit some of the assets to a family limited partnership (FLP). This way, use of the assets is possible but limited partners (or their spouses) cannot sell any of them. Distributions also can be made, depending on the desire of the general partners.

The flexibility with some of these estate planning instruments is amazing, but you just need an attorney to make sure it is all in there. You also want to be sure that one document does not clash with another — possibly making them both void — depending on what the document is for.

Children Who Do Not Want to Wait

The children may also simply be in a hurry to get their hands on the inheritance. If they are the children of the spouse to die, and he remarried, this means the children may not really know their stepmother. This could create a situation where the children may not care about the stepmother (and vice versa) and tension rises because the stepmother may want to stay in the house, but the children want what they feel should be coming to them.

Once again, if this is a possibility, then something like a bypass trust is a good solution. The stepmother cannot alter the terms of the trust, and she is entitled to the income from it until she dies.

Parents Who May Use Up Grandchildren's Estate

When you want to leave some money for your grandchildren, it is best if you create a separate instrument for them. The alternative, which is the more common method, would be to leave the money in the hands of your children. This way, however, the money may not actually get to where you want it to.

By creating a separate instrument, you do not have to wonder what will happen to it. You can make your plans and know that your intentions will be carried out. There are a number of instruments for children, but a trust will give you greater control, and for a longer period of time, if that is what you want.

27
Appointing a Trustee

Appointing a trustee puts someone or some agency that you trust in charge of the assets of a trust until the time or conditions are met by the beneficiaries. The trustee will need to be someone who is financially knowledgeable and will be responsible enough to distribute the assets of the trust as designated and as may be needed.

The selection of the trustee needs to be done with great care and in consideration of the length of time that may be involved. He or she will need to be very reliable and dedicated to the will of the grantor in fulfilling the duties. Because of the time involved, and the fact that a trustee may pass away before the trust does, a backup trustee should also be named, and terms for selecting new trustees should also be added to the trust documents.

Potential conflicts between family members when a family member is a trustee may be reduced if there is more than one trustee. This can help create a greater consensus of opinion as to how and when assets are to be distributed. Possible problems with a family member as a trustee could include a lack of financial knowledge or the fact that he or she may move and no longer be able to do the job.

With some trusts, the creator of the trust is also the trustee. This is typically the case when a living trust is used. He or she may also appoint a cotrustee to run the trust according to the preset terms when they are no longer able to do so, or simply when they do not want to.

A financial institution can also be chosen to be the trustee. These agencies do have the experience and the longevity. They also would be more costly, though, and the feasibility of it would depend on the size of the trust. It is possible that some financial institutions will only serve as trustees on a certain size trust. Another alternative, which seems to be gaining in popularity, is a kind of a compromise situation. A family member is named as the trustee, but a financial institution is appointed to be the financial advisor. Naming an agency as a financial advisor gives access to the same knowledge and experience, but will not cost as much as if they were the actual trustee of the trust.

For a trust that will last for a long time, it is important that the trustee have broader powers than with a trust that will only last a few years. The longer the time period, the greater the flexibility that will be needed, because of not being able to see what the future holds.

28
Selecting a Guardian

Part of your plans for your estate must include what is to happen to your children if you and your spouse should die, or if the surviving spouse should be incapacitated and unable to care for them. Getting your intentions recorded in a will or some other document is very important, otherwise the state may have to make the decision for you.

Choosing your children's guardians should be something that you give much thought to. There are a number of considerations that come into play as you make this choice, and some of them are:

- Which relatives are your children comfortable with?

- Which ones have children about the same age?

- Which ones have similar values and beliefs?

- Will they raise your children to believe what you believed (or at least, very similar)?

- Which ones are able to handle the task?

- Which ones have ability and willingness to do so?

- Will their age and availability make them good candidates?

- Is there a history of crime or substance abuse?

These questions are just starters to get you thinking in the right direction. The matter should not be decided hastily, and you will want to check with your relatives to make sure that they are willing to raise them for you, if needed.

It may be necessary to send your children to different homes, depending on your relatives and the ages of the children they have. In some cases, it will be necessary to provide the guardians with a maintenance allowance for the children or they may not be able to handle the additional financial drain.

Choosing another person to handle the finances for the children is a possibility if you think the guardian will not be good at that job. This is commonly done, and you may need to consider someone to handle this task as well. Be sure to name a backup in case that need should ever come.

When you name a guardian, be sure to choose one parent or the other and not name them both, in case of divorce. Also, if you and your spouse have separate wills, you want to be sure that you both have the same names selected as guardians or that part of the will gets negated and the court decides for you. You will also want to name a backup guardian in case something happens to the first choice, or they change their mind.

In the event that you become divorced, separated, or other problems come up where you do not want the other parent to raise the children, you can explain why in your will. All you need to do is detail your reasons clearly in the will and the judge will have to make a decision based on what is in the document. Although it may not be followed, it is the proper way to approach this kind of thing.

29
Helping the Financially Irresponsible

Children do not always grow up being financially responsible. There could be reasons for this, sometimes with the person himself or herself and sometimes because of other problems. Whatever the reason may be — whether emotional instability, not mentally enough developed, drug or alcohol abuse, or simply an inability or unwillingness to control spending — tools must be put into place if the estate is going to last.

The danger that lies in giving this person sudden money is that it could produce more harm than simply losing money. Even worse, is that it could be the final straw, especially in the case of substance abuse, and bring the person into the habit so deeply that there may be little chance for recovery. The money would not only be quickly lost, but it would only make the drug dealers, barkeepers, or casino operators richer.

Each situation should be handled a little differently, depending on the exact need. Here are some potential problems:

- A daughter who cannot control her spending

- A college student who thinks money grows on trees

- A son who is an alcoholic

- A spouse who regularly overspends

- A mentally retarded child

A Daughter Who Cannot Control Her Spending

When your children cannot control their spending habits, it is difficult to know what to do. On one hand, you want her to have the money, but on the other, you realize it would only end up in the pockets of the various shopkeepers, and that it would not take long to get there.

In this situation, your hard-earned money would probably not really be appreciated and it would not be spent as wisely as it should be. You want to bless her with it, but you also want to see some good come of it — for a long time to come.

One thing that you want to be careful of is finding out whether her spending habits are currently out of control. About the only way you can know for sure is to ask her outright about how she is doing financially. Ask whether she has any savings accounts or investments, whether her credit cards are maxed out, and similar questions. If there is much debt, ask what she is trying to do about it. Just because a person has a large amount of debt does not necessarily mean that spending habits are out of control. If she is trying to stop spending and is working on paying down her debt, then she may have learned the need for such control, but only after she had already accumulated the debt.

The only reason this is brought out now is because parents have an inclination to believe that spending habits of their children when they are younger may still be in practice — but change is possible. Financial maturity just comes a little slower for some than for others.

Another potential source of possible misjudgment could be if you compare your spending habits to that of your children. Times are different, costs are different, and earning potential is different. Make sure you are looking at things correctly.

If you determine that your daughter's spending habits really are out of control, then here are some options:

1. Create a trust with the following benefits:

   a. Some income to be given monthly

   b. Rewards (more money) given for earnings, wise spending, and savings

   c. Balance given at a certain age if she has learned to control spending (35, for instance)

   d. If not at 35, re-evaluation to be performed every 5 years

2. Create a trust with her children as the beneficiaries:

   a. She receives interest and a set amount each month

   b. She has no monetary control except a monthly amount

A College Student Who Thinks Money Grows on Trees

Part of your vision probably includes developing the character of your children and grandchildren. That development needs to include teaching them how to work and not be a burden to society or to others. They need to learn to carry their load.

Suppose that your youngest son has not yet learned these lessons, and you may even be wondering whether he ever will catch on. You want to leave him money for his inheritance, but he seems to have little interest or ability to understand that money represents hard work and does not come easily.

The inheritance could be used to encourage his proper handling of money. Instead of simply handing him the money, either now or when you die, a little creativity can help him to develop the traits he will need for a productive life.

Create a trust for him where the trustee is instructed to distribute the money in proportion to his earnings. You can either match his earning power with identical amounts, or give a percentage for money earned. This will quickly help him (or her) learn that rewards come with hard work and that productivity is well worth the effort.

You can let this go on until he reaches a certain age and is then evaluated by the trustee to see whether he can be trusted with the whole amount, or have the control continue until later on in life. You also may want to reward him when he completes certain college levels and maintains certain grade averages.

It needs to be pointed out, however, that alternative goals may also need to be added. Some are not cut out for college and may not be suited for particular career fields, no matter how much money you are willing to pour into them. They should not be punished simply because they do not fit into a particular mold, especially if they do learn to support themselves and live financially responsible.

A third possibility is that, in addition to the above (or instead of), you set aside some money for the start of your son's new business venture. Of course, this is an encouragement and he should know it is available if he decides to go that way. Help may be needed, though, through the counsel of a trustee, so that money and effort are not wasted, possibly leading to a quick failure if some oversight does not accompany it.

A Son Who Is an Alcoholic

This kind of situation is about the same as that of the daughter who cannot control her spending. Since you already know that much of the money given to an alcoholic (or to someone with a drug habit) will not be around for long, there must be some kind of control put on it whereby the beneficiary cannot control it or get to it.

Once again, the money needs to be put into a trust with certain stipulations placed on it. These terms should be left in the hands of the trustee to make the decision as to whether and when the son is to receive full control of the money. Using an institution as the trustee may be the safer way to go, rather than a family member.

As long as the trust creator is alive, though, he or she will want to retain control over the terms of the money in the trust for that grown child. Since even people who are on drugs or alcohol can make surprising and unexpected changes, room should be allowed for them, just in case.

Another clause needs to spell out what happens to the assets if the son never turns around. The money should then be designated toward children of that son (if there are any), but must be kept out of the reach of the son. Otherwise, it should return to the other children and be divided among them.

Tight control as to how the money can be spent should be put in place. Since alcoholics are known to even take food money from their families and spend it on alcohol, there should be no way for the son to get access to it apart from the oversight of a strong-willed trustee who can say "no." Money can be paid directly by the trustee to cover utilities, rent, food for the family members, and other essentials.

A Spouse Who Regularly Overspends

If you feel that the spouse of one of your children has a bad spending habit and you suspect he or she would probably go through your child's estate quickly, then there is some control you can exert in those kinds of situations. You can do something like in the example above where the money is placed into a trust, or a family limited partnership where all control or access to the money is removed.

How the child is to receive the money or use of the assets is determined by the trust. This form of control can be very good against creditors and will keep assets out of their hands if the mate should go deeply into debt.

If a divorce should occur, there is protection for that as well. Since only the child has the assets given to him or her, and since he or she has no direct control, there can be no way that the assets can go into the hands of the spouse. The assets will stay in the family.

A Mentally Retarded or Disabled Child

In the case of a child who is mentally retarded, or has some other debilitating illness or condition, care will need to be provided for the rest of his or her life. Steps need to be carefully taken, however, whenever any financial arrangement is made for his or her care. Taking a wrong step may totally disqualify the dependent person from being able to receive other government benefits, such as SSI or Medicaid.

Money can be put into a trust for the son or daughter, but it cannot be put in the child's name. The purpose of the trust would be to supplement the medical care and supply some personal needs. The trust will need to be set up and control over it given to someone who will be responsible and faithful to give out money as it is needed for the care of this child.

Care also needs to be taken to ensure that others do not make gifts directly to the disabled child. If a grandparent wants to make a gift, it must either go into the trust or be given to someone else on behalf of the child. Any money owned by the child could easily disqualify him or her from government benefits.

It is possible that an agency may be the best choice of a trustee, since this will probably result in the least amount of confusion. These agencies know what is needed and already understand the laws. In the event of an appointed trustee, such as another sibling, there may be confusion concerning the handling of funds, if he or she dies, until a new one can be appointed. After that, he or she may need to learn what is involved, which could create trouble in the way of continuous care.

A secondary beneficiary will also need to be named so that when the dependent son or daughter dies, the assets will then pass to the other one. Some estate planning agencies suggest that such clauses should include statements that would direct that the trust be instantly terminated if government agencies attempt to reclaim the assets on behalf of its expenditures for the child. "Spendthrift" clauses should also be there, as well, to offer further protection against these claims.

There are two kinds of guardians that may be selected for the task. As mentioned earlier, a guardian of the person is able to make medical and health decisions for the child, as well as decisions concerning where to live, education, and other such necessities. A guardian of the estate, however, only makes decisions concerning the child's finances. Both responsibilities may be in the same person, or they may be divided between two people.

There is only one type of trust that can be used to make sure that the child remains qualified to receive Medicaid. A discretionary trust leaves the disbursement of its assets up to the discretion of the trustee. If the trust should provide some kind of regular income to the child, then this most likely would disqualify him or her from receiving government benefits.

If you should leave the assets to another person, such as another sibling, to be used for the care and maintenance of the disabled child, there really is no guarantee that it will be used for such a purpose. You can get verbal agreements, but that is about all. Hopefully, he or she has the integrity to use the funds for the designated intention.

30
Protecting Against Intruders

Other things can happen, too, to ruin your plans to pass your wealth on to your heirs. One of these is creditors, which may be one of the biggest and most powerful threats to an inheritance. Creditors have access to many resources when it comes to collecting money owed to them. There are, however, several tools available that can help keep them at bay.

One of the most powerful of these is the family limited partnership (FLPs). The key to one of these, however, is that it must be set up very carefully and the principles established for it need to be diligently followed. The IRS watches over these carefully, looking for flaws in their formation and day-to-day operation. Be sure to learn more details in the section of Chapter 15 on family limited partnerships. The key is that it must have a business purpose and be run like one.

Once your business purpose is established, then the general partner (usually the parents) puts the business assets into it that they want to pass on. This greatly reduces taxes to the recipients and effectively puts all assets in the FLP. After that, the assets need to be distributed so that the limited partners, usually the children, have usage but not control over them.

When you have a son-in-law or a daughter-in-law in whom you do not want to take the risk of allowing control over the asset, then this is a good tool for that purpose. It will work well because your child has use of the assets but cannot sell it. If there should ever be a divorce, or if the spouse or your child should ever become deeply indebted to someone, the assets are beyond reach of any creditor. What can occur, however, is that any income from the FLP to that limited partner can be secured by the court and paid directly to the creditor until it is paid in full. No assets, though, can be taken away from the FLP. If there are no dividends paid out to the limited partners, then nothing can be obtained by the creditor.

The one thing that needs to be watched for is that the assets of the general partners are actually placed into the FLP and disbursed to the limited partners. You need to know that a general partner is 100 percent susceptible to creditors, except for those assets that have been distributed to the limited partners.

Another way to keep assets away from a creditor is to put the assets into a trust. You can give the beneficiary usage of the assets and distributions, but the recipient cannot have control. Once the individual has any control over the assets, then he or she may be taken to court for any debt owed to a creditor. This also applies to a husband-wife situation. For the best safety from creditors, the trust will need to be an irrevocable one. One way to do this is to designate that a grandchild is the beneficiary, but allow distributions to still be made to your son or daughter.

In the case of keeping the money from a son or daughter who is married to someone who is in debt, you may need to be very careful in your planning if you want to leave your assets to your spouse. Although you are free to transfer all of your assets to your spouse tax free, what happens after that is where problems can occur. If you want your assets to be protected from your daughter's spouse, then you will need to provide some instrument that will keep the control of those assets from that spouse's reach and from the creditor's.

If you transfer all your assets to your spouse and then leave it up to him or her to create a trust for the daughter, this could create problems. If the assets come to the children, then this could very well give the creditors access to the money, especially if it is to be owned jointly.

This is where you want to create a trust for your grandchild but leave your daughter access to the interest or other designated amount, but no direct control. This will serve to keep the assets in the family and out of the reach of creditors who may try to get access to those funds. You can also put in a clause that if there are no grandchildren at the time your daughter dies, the assets are to go to any other siblings or grandchildren and be divided equally among them.

31
Removing Heirs

Every now and then, the need can present itself to remove someone from the list of those you want to get your inheritance. Some problem, perhaps, has long been brewing and you are tired of waiting for the desired change or contact to come.

Taking someone off of your list of beneficiaries can have some serious consequences. The consequences can fall either on yourself, your spouse, or on your other children, depending on the nature of the one being cut out. So you may want to think about it a little more.

When Other Things Fail to Produce Change, Use Money

The effect of telling someone that they are "on trial" for whether or not an inheritance will come to them may be enough to bring about the desired change by itself. Perhaps it is worth a try to see whether the desired results will be brought about. Although the basic motivation here is obviously greed, for some, that may be the thing that can produce the change. You have probably already tried talking to this son, daughter, or grandchild, but found that you did not get the results you wanted. Maybe you should try it once more, but this time, tell him or her what is really at stake.

The possibility does exist that the person, if unable to sustain himself or herself, could simply transfer their burden onto the other heirs. Other solutions may be better than cutting out the person altogether. Besides that, grounds for a lawsuit may be the natural outcome. A lawsuit, even if it is not won, can have serious financial costs. It could result in the reduction of the estate by tens of thousands of dollars.

Alternatives to Disinheritance

Depending on the reason why you are considering deleting the person from your list of approved people, there may be ways to work around the problems. For instance, if it is your main concern that your son, who is an alcoholic, will spend all of your hard-earned money on alcohol, this is a problem for which there is a good solution.

You can take his part of the assets and place them in a trust. The trustee can be directed to pay your son's bills directly instead of giving money to the son. This keeps cash that could be misused out of his hands. Remember that in a trust, you are able to put in almost any terms that you want. You may even add in the possibility of a review and terms under which the money might be released to his control, such as medical evidence of proven sobriety for two or more years. Do not forget that you may not be around to make changes later. This means that any terms you want must be written in so that the trustee understands exactly what you want to do. They do not have power to alter the terms unless you write it into the trust documents.

Give Something to Everyone

The safest way to keep your estate intact and reduce the likelihood of it being challenged in court is to give something to everyone. Equal shares are even better, even if you need to put some into a trust with strict guidelines. Otherwise, leaving someone out of the will could cause legal trouble today, and the court to bypass your intentions and rewrite your estate asset divisions.

When you give something to each, this is better than totally writing someone out of the will. They cannot then go to court saying that you really wanted to include them in it — you just forgot, and the fact that you forgot shows that you were not in your right mind.

If You Must Leave Him or Her Out, Do It Right

If, after all other considerations, you find that you still cannot bring yourself to include that family member in your will, then there are definite steps you should take to provide some legal protection, which is not a guarantee, but it will help you.

You should first go to a doctor and have him or her examine you to prove that you are of sound body. Then you need to go to a psychiatrist and be verified that you are of sound mind. After that, you should make your will and have it witnessed properly and do it all on videotape. Talk freely about your decisions that are in the will, enough so that the listeners can tell that you are of a sound mind. Finally, be sure to talk about your decision as to why you are not going to include that family member who you feel you must leave out.

The details here are important. Talk with your attorney before you start the procedure or make the video, in case there are any changes in the laws where you live. Remember that there are plenty of other lawyers who will be glad to take the side of your offended family member. Following these legal procedures, however, should reduce the willingness of opposing lawyers to take up their case.

Once again, it might be simpler and save your other family members much grief if you simply leave him or her something. Remember that the assets cannot be distributed until all of the challenges are either settled or dismissed.

32
Selecting the Executor

When it comes time to select the executor of your estate, you need to give it some thought first. Some potentially large responsibilities will be involved, and you need to be sure that the one you have in mind is capable of fulfilling the role.

The task of settling an estate is not a simple one, and your choice needs to have some financial expertise and some time on their hands to be able to learn what they do not know. You should also make sure that they are willing to seek professional legal help if it should be needed. There can be a large number of responsibilities if the estate is large and complicated. Challenges to the estate could mean that it could take years to settle it all.

This makes it mandatory that you ask the person in advance whether he or she is willing to take on the role. This question should not be asked merely in passing, but you may want the individual to see what may be involved before they give you a concrete answer. One thing that would help his or her decision to be an informed one would be to meet with an attorney to answer any questions and provide a general overview of what the responsibilities may include. Here are a few of the responsibilities that an executor of a will may need to perform:

- Take title to all the assets

- Get appraised value of all assets (this may need to be submitted to the court)

- Collect all bills from creditors (including medical, and submit them to the insurance company)

- Protect assets and invest them

- Pay debts, estate and income taxes (this may include selling assets to pay them)

- Distribute the assets

You can also appoint more than one person to serve in this capacity. This is especially a good idea if the estate is large, or if you think that your primary selection could use some help. Obviously, if you choose a coexecutor, be sure that the two can work well together. You should probably avoid having very many fill this role, as it can make it more difficult to come to agreement about how things should be handled. If you do not know an able family member, or you suspect that a family member might not be the best choice (as in the case of suspecting trouble from another family member), then you can always choose an outside lawyer to handle the task.

You should also appoint a backup executor and a backup coexecutor. One or more of these appointments may not be alive when needed, or may have moved so far away that he or she would not be willing to come back to execute an estate. If there is no executor or coexecutor available, the court will need to appoint one for you.

The executor also should not have other responsibilities that may compromise this task or other ones. The executor should not be the one who also has medical powers of attorney or who can make other choices for the wealth creator. Also, he or she should not be the one who is appointed to be the guardians of the young children. Conflicts of interest may arise if he or she chooses to use money to enlarge their home for the benefit of the children, in the event that he or she receives guardianship. Then it becomes a question of where the line should be drawn.

The conditions and powers of the executor should be laid out in the will. Sometimes, an executor may even be permitted to borrow money against the estate in the event that money is needed to pay bills and taxes when no other money is available for that purpose. Also, fees for performing the duties of an executor may be allowed, but are often waived if it is a family member (this is not mandatory). There may also be limits determined by the state in which you live. Also, it may be a good idea to leave some decisions with the executor concerning how some assets are to be distributed in the event that not everything is made clear in the will.

Apart from the duties that an executor has to the estate, an executor may be held liable as a fiduciary for the estate. This means that if he or she makes financial mistakes that they could be held personally liable. This makes it necessary to move a little slower in dispersing the assets. All possible creditors need to be contacted so that accurate bills can be obtained. In most cases, there is a period of up to one year that a creditor can make a claim against the estate. If the executor distributes the assets early — and you can be sure that the family members will try to have this done — and then discovers that back taxes are due, he or she is liable for it.

33
Avoiding Mistakes That Can Destroy Your Vision

Probably the best use of your acquired wealth, no matter how great or small, is to use it to help mold and assist those who are willing and able to be useful members of society. This is what the vision is all about. You need to be aware, though, that a few simple wrong steps along the way of your planning can cause great harm in the fulfilling of your plan. In other words, mistakes can destroy much of your wealth and may hinder your intentions from being fulfilled at all.

Throughout this book, the idea has been repeated that you should get the help of professional estate planners for the legal details. In this way, you draw upon the wisdom and learning of the experts to help you create a plan that is workable and will protect much of your estate from taxes, and allow you to put your money where you want it to go. Many others run into estate planning problems when shortcuts are attempted, or when there is carelessness. Problems come in other ways, too, and here are a few of them that you want to try to avoid.

Mistake #1 - Failure to Fund the Trust or Partnership

The tools used to reduce your taxes and prevent creditors from getting hold of them are often created. Trusts are made and family limited partnerships are formed. The right documentation has been used — a lawyer has helped draw up the documents and everything else. The entities have been made that can offer a great amount of protection for your assets.

This is where many people stop, however, and the result could be disastrous. They wanted the asset protection, but unless the assets are placed into those instruments, the instruments themselves are useless. If death occurs for the grantor, it would be as if the instruments did not exist at all. Everything outside of those instruments will be thrown into the estate where they will first be reduced by estate taxes, and then creditors may also be able to get their share, too.

Usually, the failure to fund the trust or FLP is because there is an unwillingness to yield control to someone else. In a number of instruments, some control is still present, except in irrevocable trusts or outright gifts. Remember, though, that with control comes limited or almost no protection, depending on the instrument. The opposite is also true, however, that little or no control will give you the greatest level of asset protection possible for your beneficiaries.

Decisions as to what is going to go into the trusts and other instruments should be discussed with the estate planner. Time should be permitted to give it a little more thought, and then it needs to be funded quickly to provide the estate with the maximum protection. The longer an asset is left outside of your estate planning instruments, the more vulnerable it may be to others' attempts to get it.

Once an action or claim is made against the estate in some way, it is too late to make your move. An action after that would be seen simply as a way to avoid liability or hiding assets. It would also serve to make you appear even more guilty.

Mistake #2 – Leaving Everything in Your Will

Although putting all your assets into your will can direct your assets to where you want them to go, it will not provide the tax reduction you could have with even basic estate planning.

Anything that remains in your estate will be subject to at least 45 percent in taxes. This means that if you have an estate that is worth $250,000, then your estate tax will be $112,500, which will leave only $137,500. Note that this figure does not include estate taxes from your state where you live. Your heirs will probably be much happier when you pass much of the $112,500 to them, instead of to the IRS. Although the figures here are not accurate because of the personal tax exemption, these numbers will give you an idea of what the IRS will take out of your estate — almost half of it.

Leaving everything in your will does not make much sense for several reasons. The first is that a will is the easiest estate planning action to contest. Although most wills are not contested, you need to remember that the more wealth that is controlled by a will, the more likely it will be that someone may try. There are plenty of lawyers to help them, too, since they will get a portion of it if the case is won.

Good estate planning usually means taking advantage of other instruments, too, in order to avoid having your assets go through the probate system. There are many options available and methods that can suit almost any need for heirs of all ages, and also for the surviving spouse.

Care should also be taken if you are reaching your senior years. If you should die, it may hurt your spouse if there are assets given to him or her. Medicaid may be needed so that all your assets are not consumed paying for medical treatment or long-term care. This will require careful planning since Medicaid requires that assets in a trust be considered for at least five years prior to receiving any payments.

Mistake #3 – Making Impossible Demands

Your vision may have set in your mind some high goals for what your wealth can do for those who are to receive it. The truth is, however, that you need to be careful of what goals you actually place in either your will or into any trust demands.

Some goals, however noble they may appear, are not legally permissible. Not only that, but your children and grandchildren may not be so willing to go along with your plan simply because it is "your plan" and not part of their own. It could be perceived as you taking away their personal rights, depending on the nature of the demand.

Matters of Religion

Some demands, from a family point of view, and even from a religious point of view, will sound good. Some that are used rather often are such demands: "My children will receive their inheritance only if they remain in my faith," or, "They won't get a dime if they leave the faith (or marry outside of it)." While every parent desires for their children to remain in their faith, the law in this country gives them the freedom to change if they want to. So although a parent has the right to insist on continuing in the religion of their parents, nearly every court in America will deny the validity of your will because it is making demands that our laws will not uphold.

You could leave some money to the church or religious organization of your choice, and give money to your children, too.

Matters of Education

Getting a college degree could be another problem. You want to insist that your son or daughter graduate from a particular college. You went there, and now you want them to do the same. So you put it in your will that if they graduate from the college of your choosing that they can then receive their inheritance, otherwise they will not.

What if your child, however, has an accident and is not able to finish college? Is it your intention that if an unforeseen incident should occur for which they are not responsible, then they receive nothing? If you die before they graduate, then the documents remain in force as they are written. What happens if he or she is not academically gifted enough to graduate from that school, no matter how hard they may try?

Instead of making all-or-nothing statements in your will, you may want to soften the tone a little and allow room for other possible, but sometimes unforeseen, problems. Life is rarely so simple that we can predict all that might occur. Concerning college, you might promise to give a larger portion once they graduate from the school of your choice, but that you will pay for their college when they go.

Matters of Career Choice

This one usually accompanies the college choice and may even be considered the same thing. Colleges are usually chosen for the heirs along with a career field that he or she must study when they attend. Suppose, though, that your son or daughter either cannot handle it academically or has no desire to become a doctor or a lawyer? Will a decision to train for another field or vocation cause you to think less of him or her?

Though they may disappoint your high expectations, they still are your children, and they may have children, too. And the grandchildren may be able to have better lives while growing up if the parents are blessed by receiving the inheritance you have for them.

Matters of Marriage

It is more and more common today that marriages are interfaith. If you condition your child's inheritance on him or her marrying only in your faith, then you are establishing a problem for the fulfillment of your plan. The problem is that in America, people have the right to marry who they want. Therefore, a clause in your will that makes this statement would be considered void if it should be challenged. After that, your assets would be recalculated and distributed evenly to all your children, regardless of marital status.

Alternative Planning

Instead of making your demands so cut and dry, which often cannot be upheld in a court of law if put to the test, why not try to come up with a compromise solution? A little love toward your children can go a long way. Also, remember what it was like when you were their age.

Why not still give them the inheritance and allow them to draw on some of it each month, or use the assets, at least, even if you feel you cannot give them control? Let the grandchildren get the control, but let the parents have the use. This way, you do not punish your grandchildren, too, and you allow them to be raised in a better quality home and style of life.

Mistake #4 – Not Reading the Documents Before You Sign Them

As with any other legal document, a misprint can lead to trouble once you sign it. You are responsible to make sure that it conveys your intentions accurately. If you have any questions about any words used, you simply need to ask about them or look them up in a dictionary.

Mistake #5 – Trying to Save Money on Estate Planning

While most people like the idea of saving money on almost anything they can, sometimes you get what you pay for. The real problem, however, is more than just saving a little money. A slight mistake on your part, or a miscalculation, could result in losing tens of thousands of dollars or more to taxes if the estate planning documents and plans are not carefully written.

Many people try to save money by buying a do-it-yourself estate planning kit from a Web site. These documents are easy to find. The problem is that a generic document cannot provide you with the features that may be particular to your location or state. Nor can such a kit show you customized options and consider your unique situation. Legal advice is also not available, and new IRS regulations may not be included either.

Good estate planning can be costly. The more money you have, however, the more necessary it becomes to get quality estate planning. Trying to save money at the start will probably only result in throwing it away later.

You can save some money by doing some shopping around and talking to various estate planning offices. Find out their basic prices, as well as their reputation and experience. Then, once you are satisfied that one has superior performance and experience with your type of need, go with them and get your estate plan done right. Be sure to interact with your estate planner and take the time to get the full services that you are paying for, which will mean that you will need to make choices between the various options that will be presented to you. It will take some time to make a good plan, as well as repeated visits to the office, but you will have confidence in the end that it will work.

Mistake #6 – Telling Only Part of the Story

Although it may hurt to tell the whole story to your estate planner, inadequate information may prevent a thorough protection of your assets. The more that he or she knows, the more careful the planning can be. It also means a greater level of protection for your hard-earned money.

If things like mental illness, illegitimate children, or disabled children are part of your family picture, then it is best to reveal these things to the planner beforehand, rather than to have these things come up after your death and thwart your vision. Although it may not be easy to tell parts of your story, it will help to better protect your assets. Surprises can easily pop up after your death that the estate planner had no idea to prepare for, leaving part of your estate more vulnerable than it should be.

Your estate planning attorney is sworn to uphold your secrets in the utmost degree of confidence. It is better to let your planner know so that a more thorough plan can be established up front so that it may be able to withstand things that may occur later. Otherwise, you may simply be creating a loophole.

Mistake #7 – Not Keeping Your Plan Up-to-Date

Once you have paid all that money to get a good plan put in place, remember that changes in life occur that will demand updates to your plan. This includes things like new births, marriages, deaths, divorces, and much more. New assets also need to be added to your plan when they come to you.

Your estate plan should be reviewed every now and then. Then be sure to make the needed changes right away, before you forget about them. A simple thing like not updating your plan can leave some people out and may keep others in who should not be, such as your ex-spouse.

Estate plans do not update themselves, so you will need to do it. Be sure that you also put in a general clause that explains what is to be done with things not specifically mentioned in the other documents. This includes things like your household contents, jewelry, and collections.

Problems can occur if you have large amounts of things, like expensive jewelry or art, and leave them to your beneficiaries in your will. The IRS will want their share before the items are dispersed. If you have $15,000 worth of jewelry, then this tax could be as high as $8,250 (55 percent). Before you give that person the jewelry or other asset in your will, you may want to ask whether he or she will be able to pay the taxes on them. If not, then you may want to either give a smaller amount, or leave money in an insurance policy so that the tax can be paid without having to sell half of the jewelry.

When changes are made in your situation, you may need to make several changes in documents, and not just in your will. For instance, if you have life insurance policies, then you have appointed beneficiaries. A change, such as in the death of one of your children, will mean that you also need to change the beneficiary of your life insurance policy or other documents.

Mistake #8 – Making Bad Assumptions

Sometimes, when people make their plans, they automatically assume some things that they should not. If you have a farm to give to one of your children, it may be wrong to assume that a particular child would be interested. This is especially true if the child has moved away and now has a life established somewhere else and is busy with another occupation.

Other problems can be caused if the son or daughter simply has no interest in it, or has obligations that would conflict with your plans. While people do appreciate receiving things from an estate, perhaps one child might be better to receive it than another. He or she may have future plans that certain assets may hurt, rather than help. One area of concern would be in an asset that would require a good deal of time, such as a farm. This is one reason it is a good idea to at least talk to your children about your plans before you set them in stone.

Another problem could be if you own property jointly with your spouse. While this certainly works under many circumstances, there are some circumstances where it just is not a good idea by itself. If one dies first, then the other receives the assets. What happens, however, if both die at the same time? Some of these plans make no provision for the assets if this should occur. To cover it, you need to have the details spelled out in your will, or in both wills if each spouse has one.

Another assumption often made is that since you are giving your heirs valuable assets and property, they should be happy. While they probably will be happy when they receive the news, that happiness could quickly turn to sorrow if they have to sell it in order to be able to pay the taxes on it. Remember that taxes and debts must be paid before the inheritance can be disbursed. If you know that being able to pay the taxes could be a problem with an heir, then you will also need to leave enough cash on hand to cover this expense, or the property will have to be sold or the money borrowed.

One way to ensure that your heirs have enough to pay all taxes and debts is to provide a life insurance policy for this purpose. Be sure to also include enough of a maintenance amount for your spouse and any dependent children that will cover them for at least two years. Settling an estate could take up to three years if there are any challenges or other problems.

One more assumption that is made too often is that a parent may count on one child to give part of the inheritance given to him or her to another child. In other words, the one child becomes responsible for sharing the estate. If it is in words only, then there is no force available to make it happen. Although the one child may be responsible enough to carry it out, others that are not so inclined, such as a spouse, may come to bring pressure on him or her. Documents are available to ensure that your plan is carried out, but you need to use some care in preparing it. Advice from an estate planner will go a long way toward fulfilling your estate plan.

34
Business Matters

When you have a business in the family, it can present a number of challenges to the estate planner, some good and some bad, depending on whether most of the assets are tied up in it. The larger the percentage of the assets in the business, and the more children there are, the more complicated it can become. This problem can be minimal, however, if there is only one child.

The problem occurs because children often want their inheritance when it becomes available. One son may want to run the business, but a brother and a sister may want the cash. Your will needs to be specific concerning the family business so that difficulties are reduced and divisions are made easier. Unspecified directions involved with a family business can only mean trouble between the children when decisions need to be made. It is better to have those details worked out in advance.

For instance, if you leave no details or options in your will, children who want the cash may force the hand of him or her who wants to continue to run the business. This means that it would need to be sold, unless an alternative arrangement can be made. If it is a cash-producing business, then other alternatives could be made. The one may buy out those who simply want cash, or the land may be given to those wanting the cash, and the business then simply pays rent until the inheritance is equaled.

In other situations, the executor may need to take an active role in the leadership of the business, since it falls on his or her shoulders to ensure that the estate retains, and even gains, value if possible. This means that some family members may come to resent him or her, especially if he or she has little real-world business experience or knowledge.

Another difficulty that the executor of the will faces is the decision of how to deal with the business itself. If the business is doing well before the owner dies, that is no guarantee that it will continue to do so. In fact, if it fails to do so, then the blame could fall on the executor. This could be why many executors like to try and sell the business as soon as possible.

If the business continues to do well, then taxes should not be a problem. If the business takes a dive, however, the same amount of taxes will be due, but the business could now have great difficulty paying them.

The owner of the business, the estate creator, should have plans in existence already, or will need to create them, as to what should happen to the business in the event of his or her death. These plans should be relevant to the estate planning, and should show what happens to it and how it is to be run, until the heirs can make decisions concerning its future. Without these being in place, the business could become worthless in a short time, leaving the heirs with nothing except bills.

If the owner intends to hand the business over to one of the children, then that child should be getting prepared. This means that there should be a familiarity with the business and its daily operation in order to ensure the least interruption and to maintain its value. There may also need to be some specialized education required if it is a larger business or if the business is of a technical nature.

Selling the business can be done in a number of ways to make the transition smooth. One of these ways would be to let the employees buy it. It may even be better, however, for the owner to settle what happens to it before he or she dies.

It is also possible that co-owners will want to buy out the share of the deceased, freeing up the assets and the business from the family control. To make this step go smoother, the co-owners should draw up documents as to the value of each other's part in the business and the price necessary for a buyout by the other partners. This way, no complicated calculation process will need to take place after the death, except possibly to bring it more up to date. This will also eliminate some possible surprises, if the current partners want to give a low estimate.

If there are already family members in the business, and they are the ones who actually make it run and profit, they probably will resent it if any family members receive distributions from it who are not involved in it. Selling the business and giving cash to each of the heirs may be the best way to go in some cases.

In other cases, if there are other assets, equal value could be given to each of the children, equalizing their inheritance. Another possibility would be to buy insurance of equal value, and when you die, the child receives his or her inheritance tax free, as long as it does not go into the estate.

Insurance could be purchased ahead of time on each of the partners so that a buyout can take place in the event of one of the partners' death. This would enable the business to continue without interruption or threats to its existence if family members want their cash. A possible alternative would be to create a savings account that would build up enough to buy out one partner or another in the event of wanting out, or death.

Selling your business to your children may create some serious tax problems. Taxes will be based upon the current value of the business, which could place this way beyond the ability of the son or daughter to pay, especially if it has been successful. Another option is for the parents to give the business to the children and claim the annual gift limits each year of $12,000 per person. In return, the children would give the parents an annual salary and make payments on the business to the parents and to any other siblings.

Conclusion
The Uncertain Future of Estate Planning

Ever since Congress passed legislation with an increased gift and estate tax, it has been known that the day would come when it would affect everyone who has an estate plan. Although estate planners have done what they could, we still do not know what will happen in 2010 — whether Congress will pass new legislation that will bring about the desired results or whether the estate tax will drop back down to the $1 million personal exemption limit of 2001.

What this means for you is that within the next couple of years, you will need to be in close touch with your estate planner to ensure that your estate plan is up to date and will help protect your estate against those unwanted taxes.

A total rearrangement of your finances may be necessary, or perhaps no changes will be needed at all. At this point, it is hard to tell. You may even want to get in touch with your Congressman or Congresswoman to help push the right legislation through.

Chances are good, though, that new laws will be enacted that will still provide a good deal of protection for those who need it. It could end up being even better than it will be in 2009, with $7 million per couple in personal exemption being available. People in Congress, as well as people in business, will surely be screaming loudly for the new legislation.

Bibliography

Baker, Sandy. *The Complete Guide to Planning Your Estate: A Step-by-Step Plan to Protect Your Assets, Limit Your Taxes, and Ensure Your Wishes Are Fulfilled.* Ocala, FL: Atlantic Pubsihing Group, 2007.

Condon, Gerald M., Esq., and Condon, Jeffrey L., Esq. *Beyond the Grave: The Right Way and the Wrong Way of Leaving Money to Your Children (and Others).* New York: HarperBusiness, 2001.

Fish, Barry, and Kotzer, Les. *The Family Fight: Planning to Avoid It.* Washington, D.C.: Continental Atlantic, 2002.

Hughes, James E., Jr. *Family Wealth: Keeping It in the Family.* Princeton, NJ: Bloomberg Press, 2004.

Lucas, Stuart E. *Wealth: Grow It, Protect It, Spend It, and Share It.* Upper Saddle River, NJ: Wharton, 2006.

Williams, Roy, and Preisser, Vic. *Preparing Heirs: Five Steps to a Successful Transition of Family Wealth and Values.* San Francisco: Robert D. Reed, 2003.

Biography

Mike Valles is a freelance financial writer who writes about almost anything dealing with financial matters. Mostly writing as a "ghost," he has written hundreds of articles and many eBooks that are now circulating around the Web. His first contact with estate planning was to write articles about them for lawyers. Ever since, his interest has greatly expanded as he saw an increased need for this knowledge to be circulated to wider circles. It was that information that led to the creation of this book.

He has clients around the globe that he has written for and enjoys putting words in an easy-to-understand way so that the average person can grasp it. He loves writing and communicating ideas about useful things.

He currently lives in beautiful Tennessee with his wife, and one son still at home. Being an ordained minister, he also continues to teach and preach as he is able to do so. For a number of years he has taught college-level courses related to the Bible and various theological themes. He also enjoys writing about these same themes as well.

Index